S0-BRS-594

**At Issue**

| Organic Food

# Other Books in the At Issue Series:

# At Issue

# Organic Food

*Amy Francis, Book Editor*

**GREENHAVEN PRESS**
*A part of Gale, Cengage Learning*

GALE
CENGAGE Learning·

Farmington Hills, Mich • San Francisco • New York • Waterville, Maine
Meriden, Conn • Mason, Ohio • Chicago

Patricia Coryell, *Vice President & Publisher, New Products & GVRL*
Douglas Dentino, *Manager, New Products*
Judy Galens, *Acquisitions Editor*

*For more information, contact:*
Greenhaven Press
27500 Drake Rd.
Farmington Hills, MI 48331-3535
Or you can visit our Internet site at gale.cengage.com

For product information and technology assistance, contact us at

Gale Customer Support, 1-800-877-4253
For permission to use material from this text or product, submit all requests online at www.cengage.com/permissions.

Further permissions questions can be e-mailed to permissionrequest@cengage.com.

Articles in Greenhaven Press anthologies are often edited for length to meet page requirements. In addition, original titles of these works are changed to clearly present the main thesis and to explicitly indicate the author's opinion. Every effort is made to ensure that Greenhaven Press accurately reflects the original intent of the authors. Every effort has been made to trace the owners of copyrighted material.

Cover photograph copyright © Debra Hughes 2007. Used under license from Shutterstock .com.

LIBRARY OF CONGRESS CATALOGING-IN-PUBLICATION DATA

Organic food / Amy Francis, book editor.
    pages cm. -- (At issue)
    Includes bibliographical references and index.
    ISBN 978-0-7377-7181-7 (hardcover) -- ISBN 978-0-7377-7182-4 (pbk.)
    1. Natural foods 2. Organic farming 3. Internet and teenagers--Juvenile literature. I. Francis, Amy.
    TX369.O647 2015
    641.3'02--dc23
                                                              2014034677

Printed in Mexico
1 2 3 4 5 6 7 19 18 17 16 15

# Contents

# Introduction

In March 2007, several varieties of pet food imported from China were recalled due to melamine discovered in the products. It was later found that the melamine was intentionally added to two ingredients, wheat gluten and rice protein, to make it appear the products contained more protein than they actually did. Although there is no database to track illnesses caused by pet food, thousands of pets are believed to have died from melamine-related kidney failure as a result of the tainted food. This wouldn't be the last time China and melamine would make headlines.

In mid-July 2008, melamine was found again, but this time in watered-down milk in China, which was used in the production of infant formula. There were approximately three hundred thousand cases of illness in young children and several deaths resulted. As in the pet food incident, it was later discovered that the melamine was added intentionally.

As these stories made headlines around the world, many in the media expressed concern over food from China entering the world food supply. On November 14, 2008, the US Food and Drug Administration (FDA) issued an alert against all finished food products from China. As of July 2014, the FDA lists seventy-nine active alerts for specific Chinese products with concerns ranging from "filth" in seafood to candies containing lead.

Regardless of these incidents, the flow of imported foods coming from China into the United States has not abated. In fact, Chinese imports continued to increase annually. According to Food and Water Watch, China produced 80 percent of the tilapia, 51 percent of the cod, and 50 percent of the apple juice Americans consumed in 2011. The US Department of Agriculture reports the United States imported 4.1 billion pounds of food from China in 2012.

Adding to the problem is that the US government doesn't have the resources to inspect all these food imports. As Stanley Lubman pointed out in the *Wall Street Journal*, due to the large amount of imported goods, it is nearly impossible to avoid foods that originated in China, and FDA inspectors cover "a mere 2.3 percent of the total of all imported food products."[1]

Further, China is far from being the only country of concern exporting food to the United States. In one case, as Rick Schmitt reported on Minnpost.com, US investigators at a seafood company in southern India found "water tanks rife with microbiological contamination, rusty carving knives, peeling paint above the work area, unsanitary bathrooms and an outdoor ice machine covered with insects."[2] The FDA issued an "import alert," but 425 people across the United States were already sick from salmonella traced back to the seafood company.

The list goes on. Vanilla from several producers in Mexico, dried preserved fruit products from Hong Kong, and pesticide residue on papaya from Belize, apples from Brazil, sweet potatoes from Jamaica, and even some grapes from Canada. In all, the FDA's extensive "import alert" list includes alerts for producers from over 150 countries.

With this in mind, one might think imported food poses the greatest threat to the US food supply; however, the worst outbreaks of food-born illness resulting in death recorded in the United States weren't linked to foreign imports. Instead the most recent problem, in 2011, originated from cantaloupe contaminated with listeria monocytogenes that was grown on a Colorado farm. As a result, thirty people died and 146 addi-

---

1. Stanley Lubman, "Why Americans Should Worry About China's Food Safety Problems," *Wall Street Journal*, May 21, 2013. http://blogs.wsj.com/chinarealtime/2013/05/21/why-americans-should-worry-about-chinas-food-safety-problems.
2. Rick Schmitt, "As More Imported Foods Reach the Dinner Table, Holes Remain in FDA Safety Net," Minnpost.com, June 27, 2014. http://www.minnpost.com/politics-policy/2014/06/more-imported-foods-reach-dinner-table-holes-remain-fda-safety-net.

tional cases of illness from the cantaloupe were recorded. This incident was second only to a 1985 listeria outbreak from cheese manufactured in California. In that instance, fifty-two people died. In yet another food-poisoning case in early 2009, contaminated peanut butter resulted in nine deaths and over twenty-two thousand cases of illness.

Still, even with all of these food safety issues combined, there may be an even bigger food-related threat in the United States. Melanie Warner, writing in The Daily Beast, compared the three thousand annual deaths from food-borne illness to the 310,000 Americans who die from diet-related conditions such as diabetes, obesity, and heart disease. She writes, "The big problem with our food supply isn't pathogens, it is processed food. We're being killed not by E. coli, salmonella, or campylobacter, but by the nutritionally hollow contents of the bags, boxes, and fast-food clamshells that have managed to pass as nourishment in our society."[3]

Sticking with whole foods and plenty of fresh fruits and vegetables may be the one area of consensus among most nutritionists, but when it comes to choosing the best products, there is still plenty of disagreement. The value of organic foods to our health, the health of farm workers, and health of our planet is debated in the following pages of At Issue: Organic Food.

3. Melanie Warner, "Our Unsafe Food Supply Is Killing Us," The Daily Beast, March 1, 2013. www.thedailybeast.com/articles/2013/03/01/our-unsafe-food-supply-is-killing-us.html.

# 1

# Organic Food Is Worth the Extra Cost

*Brian Fung*

*Brian Fung is the technology writer at* National Journal. *He was previously an associate editor at* The Atlantic *and has written for* Foreign Policy *and* The Washington Post.

*Studies out of Stanford University show organic food is not nutritionally superior to conventionally grown food. While these studies were widely publicized and discussed among the public, their focus was off mark. The reason choosing organic products is so important is not because they are more nutritious but because choosing organic reduces pesticide exposure to the consumer, farm workers, and the environment. Although organic may not be nutritionally superior, it is still worth the additional cost.*

Of all the food-related countercultural buzzwords that have gone mainstream in recent years, *organic* ranks among the most confusing. Like its cousins (cf. [compare] *local, free-range,* or worst of all, *natural*), the term's promotion by grocery stores everywhere has caused it to escape the strict definitions laid out by the USDA [US Department of Agriculture]. But from Stanford University comes new research suggesting what we should have known all along: organic food isn't actually more nutritious than traditionally-farmed goods.

In a widely publicized and discussed analysis of more than 200 studies comparing organic to regular food products, researchers have found that organics don't have more vitamins or minerals (with the lone exception of phosphorus, which we all get in sufficient amounts anyway). Nor do they have an appreciable effect when it comes to heading off food-borne illness, although the germs found in conventional meat do have a higher chance of being drug-resistant (more on that in a bit).

That we needed a study to understand how nutritionally similar organic foods are to non-organics is a perfect example of the way we've lost sight of what the term really means. It's worth keeping in mind that *organic* refers only to a particular method of production; while switching to organic foods can be good for you insofar as doing so helps you avoid nasty things like chemicals and additives, there's nothing in the organic foods themselves that gives them an inherent *nutritional* advantage over non-organics. In other words, it's not wrong to say organic food is "healthier" than non-organics. It's just unrealistic to think that your organic diet is slowly turning you into Clark Kent.

---

*For all the attention devoted to the ways organic is better for you, we should remember that* organic *began chiefly as an argument about the environment.*

---

(You laugh, but according to a Nielsen study cited by *USA Today*, a ton of people believe just that, or something close to it. Fifty-one percent of those surveyed said they bought organic food because they thought it was more nutritious.)

Still, there are important reasons beyond nutrition to choose organic foods. Let's start at the source: USDA rules prohibit food makers from labeling something organic unless it can prove that at least 95 percent of a product was made using organic processes, which are themselves defined as:

A production system that is managed in accordance with the Act and regulations in this part to respond to site-specific conditions by integrating cultural, biological, and mechanical practices that foster cycling of resources, promote ecological balance, and conserve biodiversity.

For all the attention devoted to the ways organic is better for you, we should remember that *organic* began chiefly as an argument about the environment. From the agency's perspective, to buy organic is to respect the land your food came from. It means taking pains to ensure that your farms remain bountiful and productive, even decades from now. The case is one part self-interest over the long term, and one part a statement of ethics. Not really what you'd expect from a mechanical bureaucratic institution.

## Organic Foods and Public Health

Buying organic is also a statement about public health. Nowhere is this clearer than in the case of antibiotics. Conventional farms have been putting the stuff in animal feed for decades—even though we've known since the 1970s about the health hazards that the animal use of antibiotics poses for humans. Reducing society's chances of inadvertently creating a superbug is a good reason to purchase organic foods.

There are the more immediate health benefits of buying organic: you'll avoid the chemicals, preservatives, and hormones that conventional farms often use to treat their foods. In the Stanford study, just 7 percent of organic foods were found to have traces of pesticides, compared to 38 percent of conventionally-farmed produce. Again, that doesn't mean organic foods will supercharge your health—you'll just be at less risk of exposure to potentially harmful substances, for whatever that's worth to you. Quantifying that benefit is a contentious area and certainly worthy of more research.

And then there's the reason many people find most compelling of all: the health of workers in the field. For some consumers, buying organic is a human-rights issue. Reading *Atlantic* contributor Barry Estabrook's *Tomatoland* on the ruinous health problems of tomato planters and pickers in Florida because of the use of herbicides and pesticides is enough to make almost anyone choose organic over non-organic. Yes, there are safety rules in place for the use of these lethal chemicals, but as Estabrook's work and the work of others shows, those rules are frequently not followed.

Even if organic foods may not be uniquely nutritionally fortified as many of us have grown accustomed to thinking, don't write them off just yet. They still mean a great deal. And besides—it seems unfair to judge organic crops for failing to do something they never claimed to be capable of in the first place. They're simply the victims of our projection.

# 2

# Eating Organic Food Isn't that Much Healthier, Study Finds

**New York Post**

*The* New York Post *is an American daily newspaper and a digital news outlet that includes nypost.com and pagesix.com.*

*The demand for organic products continues to rise despite the high cost. Many consumers of organic foods believe they are getting a superior product. A recent study from Stanford University, however, showed organic food has no added nutritional benefit. Although organic produce contains lower levels of pesticides, pesticides found on conventionally grown produce are well within safe limits. Those who are concerned about pesticide consumption should focus instead on produce grown in North America where levels tend to be lower.*

Patient after patient asked: Is eating organic food, which costs more, really better for me?

Unsure, Stanford University doctors dug through reams of research to find out—and concluded there's little evidence that going organic is much healthier, citing only a few differences involving pesticides and antibiotics.

Eating organic fruits and vegetables can lower exposure to pesticides, including for children—but the amount measured from conventionally grown produce was within safety limits, the researchers reported Monday.

Nor did the organic foods prove more nutritious.

"I was absolutely surprised," said Dr. Dena Bravata, a senior research affiliate at Stanford and long-time internist who began the analysis because so many of her patients asked if they should switch.

"There are many reasons why someone might choose organic foods over conventional foods," from environmental concerns to taste preferences, Bravata stressed. But when it comes to individual health, "there isn't much difference."

Her team did find a notable difference with antibiotic-resistant germs, a public health concern because they are harder to treat if they cause food poisoning.

Specialists long have said that organic or not, the chances of bacterial contamination of food are the same, and Monday's analysis agreed. But when bacteria did lurk in chicken or pork, germs in the non-organic meats had a 33 percent higher risk of being resistant to multiple antibiotics, the researchers reported Monday in the journal *Annals of Internal Medicine*.

---

*Consumers can pay a lot more for some organic products but demand is rising: Organic foods accounted for $31.4 billion sales last year.*

---

That finding comes amid debate over feeding animals antibiotics, not because they're sick but to fatten them up. Farmers say it's necessary to meet demand for cheap meat. Public health advocates say it's one contributor to the nation's growing problem with increasingly hard-to-treat germs. Caroline Smith DeWaal, food safety director at the Center for Science in the Public Interest, counted 24 outbreaks linked to multidrug-resistant germs in food between 2000 and 2010.

The government has begun steps to curb the nonmedical use of antibiotics on the farm.

Organic foods account for 4.2 percent of retail food sales, according to the U.S. Department of Agriculture. It certifies products as organic if they meet certain requirements including being produced without synthetic pesticides or fertilizers, or routine use of antibiotics or growth hormones.

Consumers can pay a lot more for some organic products but demand is rising: Organic foods accounted for $31.4 billion sales last year, according to a recent Obama administration report. That's up from $3.6 billion in 1997.

The Stanford team combed through thousands of studies to analyze the 237 that most rigorously compared organic and conventional foods. Bravata was dismayed that just 17 compared how people fared eating either diet while the rest investigated properties of the foods themselves.

Organic produce had a 30 percent lower risk of containing detectable pesticide levels. In two studies of children, urine testing showed lower pesticide levels in those on organic diets. But Bravata cautioned that both groups harbored very small amounts—and said one study suggested insecticide use in their homes may be more to blame than their food.

Still, some studies have suggested that even small pesticide exposures might be risky for some children, and the Organic Trade Association said the Stanford work confirms that organics can help consumers lower their exposure.

CSPI's DeWaal noted that difference, but added that the issue is more complicated. Some fruits and vegetables can harbor more pesticide residue than others—she listed peaches from Chile as topping a recent testing list. Overall levels have dropped in North American produce over the last decade as farms implemented some new standards addressing child concerns, she said.

"Parents with young children should consider where their produce is coming from," DeWaal said, calling types grown in the U.S. or Canada "a safer bet" for lower pesticide levels.

As for antibiotics, some farms that aren't certified organic have begun selling antibiotic-free meat or hormone-free milk, to address specific consumer demands, noted Bravata. Her own preference is to buy from local farmers in hopes of getting the ripest produce with the least handling.

That kind of mixed approach was evident in a market in the nation's capital Thursday, where Liz Pardue of Washington said she buys organic "partially for environmental reasons." Pardue said she doesn't go out of her way to shop organic, but if she does, it's to buy mostly things that are hard to wash like berries and lettuce.

Michelle Dent of Oxon Hill, Md., said she buys most of her groceries from regular chain stores but gets her fruit from organic markets: "It's fresh; you can really taste it."

Anna Hamadyk of Washington said she buys only organic milk because she has a young son.

"I would love to buy everything organic, but it's just too much money," said Hamadyk, who also shops at local farmers markets.

# 3

# Pesticides Are Poisoning the Human Population

*Maria Rodale*

*Maria Rodale is the chief executive officer and chairman of Rodale, Inc., an independent publisher of health, wellness, and environmental content.*

*Thousands of pounds of various chemicals, many of which have not undergone sufficient testing or are already known carcinogens, are sprayed onto US fields and fed to farm animals every week. Although government agencies assure all the chemicals used in food production are safe in small amounts, there are no safe limits when it comes to ingesting pesticides. In some cases, small amounts may even be more damaging, and rates of attention deficit hyperactivity disorder (ADHD), asthma, diabetes, food allergies, and other health issues have steadily climbed along with their use. The government can do more to protect the land and the American people. Chemicals used in food production are destroying humans and their use must be stopped.*

We have been conditioned to fear many things, especially what is different from us. We are afraid of bugs, bacteria, and things that are scary, so we kill them. We have yet to make the connection that in killing other things we are also killing ourselves.

Maria Rodale, "Chapter 2: We Have Poisoned Ourselves and Our Children," *Organic Manifesto: How Organic Farming Can Heal Our Planet, Feed the World, and Keep Us Safe*, Rodale Books, 2010. Copyright © 2010 by Maria Rodale. Permission granted by Rodale, Inc., Emmaus, PA 18098.

The environmental impact of agricultural chemicals alone is, to my mind, sufficient scientific and ethical argument for putting an end to their use. But agricultural chemicals such as pesticides, fertilizers, herbicides, and their household counterparts are destroying more than soil and water.

Like many people, I am worried about our climate crisis. But in certain locations, you can imagine a future where global warming is not that bad. It might mean warm weather all the time, new beachfront properties, and growing citrus trees or coffee plants in Pennsylvania. And if you are truly honest with yourself, saving the polar bear might not make your top 10 list of things to do this year. It is heartbreaking to watch mother polar bears and their babies drowning because they can't swim far enough to reach ice or land. But it is so far away and feels so hard to address. Maybe you write a check and feel better, but that doesn't really change much.

## Chemical Exposure and Health

Meanwhile, autism and attention-deficit/hyperactivity disorder (ADHD), diseases virtually unheard of a few decades ago, are now diagnosed regularly. Of every 100 children born today, one will be diagnosed with autism before the age of 8. About 4.4 million children between the ages of 4 and 17 have been diagnosed with ADHD. Rates of asthma, diabetes, and childhood obesity are at all-time highs and scientists can't explain why the number of children with food allergies has increased 18 percent in the last decade. Is it a coincidence that the prevalence of these problems has increased as we have increased the use of chemicals to grow our food?

Experts might claim that our reporting and diagnostic technologies are better than they used to be, which is probably true. But compared to other countries where the reporting is just as good (if not better), we in the United States spend far more on health care, but have dismal results. Our life expectancy is the shortest and our infant mortality rate is the highest of any developed nation. In many of the countries whose citizens have longer life spans than Americans do, a lot of the chemicals that we believe are necessary to grow food have already been banned.

On his way out of office, President George W. Bush halted the program that tests pesticide levels on fruits, vegetables, and field crops because the cost—$8 million a year—is "too expensive." That's just one small example of where our priorities are when it comes to protecting our health and that of our children.

---

*The Union of Concerned Scientists has repeatedly warned of a link between [methicillin-resistant* Staphylococcus aureus] *and the overuse of antibiotics on large hog farms.*

---

According to the Mount Sinai Medical Center Children's Environmental Health Center (CEHC) in New York City, more than 80,000 new chemical compounds have been introduced since World War II [1939–1945]. Many of them are used in agriculture. There are 3,000 so-called high-production-volume chemicals, meaning that more than 1 million pounds of each are produced or imported in the United States each year. More than 2.5 billion tons of these chemicals are released into the environment in the United States alone *each year.* In addition, more than 4 billion pounds of pesticides are used annually in the United States—to kill everything from agricultural pests to inner-city cockroaches to microbes and bacteria in schools and hospitals. Traces of all of these chemicals can be detected in virtually each and every one of us. Yet only half of the compounds have been even minimally tested and less than 20 percent have been tested for their effects on fetal nervous systems. (What parent would *agree* to that sort of testing in the first place? And yet all of our children have already been exposed.) At least 75 percent of the manufactured chemical compounds that *have* been tested are known to cause cancer and are toxic to the human brain.

"Failure to test chemicals for toxicity represents a grave lapse of stewardship," says Philip Landrigan, MD, professor and chairman of the CEHC. "It reflects a combination of industry's unwillingness to take responsibility for the products they produce coupled with failure of the US government to require toxicity testing of chemicals in commerce." . . .

## Cheap Food Equals High Health-Care Costs

To feed our demand for cheap food, we have put ourselves and especially our children's lives at risk. According to an article in the *Archives of Otolaryngology*, there has been an "alarming" increase in drug-resistant infections in children— especially in the ears, sinuses, head, and throat (tonsils). In the period between 2001 and 2006, MRSA (methicillin-resistant *Staphylococcus aureus*) head and neck infections caused by drug-resistant bacteria in children have more than doubled— from 12 percent in 2001 to 28 percent in 2006. Dr. Landrigan attributes this increasing resistance to overuse of antibiotics in raising our food. When asked if he sees increased incidence of drug-resistant infections in his own practice in New York City, he replies that it is "all over the place" and it "worries the hell out of me."

Dr. Landrigan has good reason to be worried. MRSA affects children and healthy adults. It had been confined to hospitals, but now you can catch MRSA at gyms, schools, day care centers, and military barracks. The Union of Concerned Scientists has repeatedly warned of a link between MRSA and the overuse of antibiotics on large hog farms. A peer-reviewed study in *Applied and Environmental Microbiology* confirmed that MRSA is found on almost half the pork and 20 percent of beef samples taken from a sampling of 30 supermarkets in Louisiana. The European Union, South Korea, and many other countries prohibit preventive use of antibiotics in the factories where animals are raised for meat. Not in the United States. In fact, farmers can just go to their local farm stores to buy a 50-pound bag of antibiotics—without a prescription.

In response to the spiraling rise of bacterial and viral infections, many concerned parents, hospitals, and schools have begun indiscriminately using antibacterial products. But those very products are part of the problem. Think of it this way: *You and your kids are washing your hands in pesticides.* The EPA [US Environmental Protection Agency] recently allowed triclosan, the predominant antibacterial agent used in products from shampoo to water bottles to crib liners, to be re-registered [chemicals need to go through a periodic re-registration process in which all of their risks are reviewed], even though the EPA acknowledges that triclosan interacts with androgen and estrogen receptors and affects the thyroid gland in rats. The EPA acknowledges that triclosan is linked to antibiotic resistance, and that it is showing up in fish and drinking water. The EPA doesn't have to look at triclosan again until 2013.

The Endocrine Society was founded in 1916 to research the role of hormones on our health. It recently released a major report to raise concern about the effects of chemicals, including the organochlorinated pesticides, on our health. "In this first Scientific Statement of The Endocrine Society, we present the evidence that endocrine disruptors have effects on male and female reproduction, breast development and cancer, prostate cancer, neuroendocrinology, thyroid, metabolism and obesity, and cardiovascular endocrinology. Results from animal models, human clinical observations, and epidemiological studies converge to implicate EDCs [endocrine-disrupting chemicals] as a significant concern to public health." The Endocrine Society also validated what is known as the low-dose or inverse dose response factor, which means that *any* dose—even small ones—have the potential to do major damage. The statement also called attention to the direct link that the Agricultural Health Study has found between increased prostate cancer rates, methyl bromide (a fungicide used heavily on strawberries, among other crops), and many pesticides.

While "endocrine" seems like a fairly nonthreatening term, there is one endocrine disease we are all familiar with: diabetes. Endocrine disruptors include the organophosphate pesticides, atrazine, bisphenol A, lead, mercury, and many other common chemicals we ingest daily—though we don't intend to.

Dr. Simon Baron-Cohen has a hypothesis about autism that's called "the extreme male theory," which theorizes that a hormonal imbalance leads to "overmasculinization" of a child's brain. Harvey Karp, MD, a world-renowned pediatrician, recently proposed that exposure to endocrine disrupters might be the cause.

---

*It's truly an outrage that our government has not done more to prevent the use of these known carcinogens.*

---

Diabetes and autism are both increasing to epidemic proportions. Until recently, synthetic chemicals have escaped blame.

## Known Carcinogens

What about cancer? Despite investing billions and billions of dollars in research money, cancer death rates have remained fairly flat since the 1950s. Two well-researched books, *The Secret History of the War on Cancer* by Devra Davis, PhD, and *The Politics of Cancer Revisited* by Samuel S. Epstein, MD, reveal that experts have known since the 1930s about the connection between environmental toxins, hormones, and cancer. And yet, as Dr. Davis documents in her book, the companies that fund lobbying groups have actively suppressed information, infiltrated and run the charitable organizations that are supposed to cure them, and invested in huge advertising campaigns to create a public sense of confidence in the very companies that are withholding and perverting the truth.

"In America and England, one out of every two men and one out of every three women will develop cancer in their lifetime," Dr. Davis writes. "Cancer is the leading killer of middle-aged persons, and, after accidents, the second-leading killer of children." Both she and Dr. Epstein list as irrefutable causes of cancer pesticides, including atrazine and arsenic; hormones, including artificial growth hormones that are used on animals; and the thousands of chemicals (and plastics) that are hormone disruptors. It's truly an outrage that our government has not done more to prevent the use of these known carcinogens. . . .

---

*Just because a toxic chemical is scientifically proven to be harmful doesn't guarantee that our government will respond in a way that protects us.*

---

## No Safe Level

Dr. Warren Porter is no stranger to the chemical companies or the EPA. Many years ago, despite threats from chemical companies, he and his colleagues published a study showing that aldicarb (an N-methyl carbamate), an insecticide commonly applied to citrus, cotton, potatoes, and watermelon crops and added to irrigation water, is a powerful immune suppressant. That means it reduces your body's ability to fight off disease. The greatest effects were at the lowest doses (1 part per billion), 100 times lower than the EPA's safety standard. Rather than remove aldicarb from the market as a result of that study, the EPA ceased funding Dr. Porter's research. Aldicarb is still used heavily today. In fact, it was the chemical that in 1984 caused the disaster at Bhopal, India, killing thousands of Indians instantly and leaving more than 100,000 chronically ill, deformed, and in pain. (Check out http://bhopal.org for the full horror story.) But you don't need a manufacturing plant explosion to cause damage. Scientists, including Dr. Porter and Dr. Landrigan, are all seeing the inverse dose response to many chemicals—from aldicarb to lead. They have found that in some cases *smaller doses actually do more harm than larger doses*. This flies in the face of all the government standards that set "allowable safe limits" to chemical exposures. In a scientific paper published in 2003, Wayne Welshons and colleagues demonstrated that at low concentrations of estrogen-mimicking chemicals, the EPA model for assessing biological effects *underestimated* those effects by a factor of 10,000. There are no safe limits, no matter how small. As Dr. Landrigan says about lead, "the biggest bang for the buck still occurs at the lowest doses."

Larger doses, of course, cause death.

In 2002, Porter and colleagues published a paper showing that a weed killer commonly used on lawns that includes 2,4-D caused abortions and absorption of fetuses. A representative from a chemical company that sells this product approached a dean at his university and demanded that the paper be retracted. The dean replied that the peer-review process would settle any concerns and, thankfully, responsible scientific process prevailed since there was no credible scientific evidence presented to counter the data in their paper. Yet products that contain 2,4-D remain the most commonly used herbicides in the world today, with more than 46 million pounds applied in the United States every year. Once again, just because a toxic chemical is scientifically proven to be harmful doesn't guarantee that our government will respond in a way that protects us.

Porter's 1999 study shows how atrazine and nitrates in drinking water can alter the aggression levels, thyroid hormone levels, and immune systems of mice. It's not good. Many studies have shown that atrazine, one of the herbicides most commonly used in the United States, is an endocrine disruptor, which has demasculinized frogs, caused mutations in the frogs' testes and ovaries, diminished their essential ability to call for a mate, damaged sperm quality in frogs and possibly humans, and contaminated groundwater. The European Union banned atrazine in 2003, yet more than 76 million pounds are applied in the United States each year. In 2006, the EPA issued a statement declaring that the use of atrazine posed no threat to the US population, including children and infants. It based this conclusion on the results of a few studies done by Syngenta, the maker of atrazine. Although Syngenta is a Swiss company, it has a very large US business. (In 2005, the Natural Resources Defense Council, a nonprofit advocacy group, sued the EPA over what it called "backroom deals with pesticide makers" like Syngenta.) When you look up atrazine on the Office of Ground Water and Drinking Water section of the EPA's Web site, it attributes these health effects to short-term exposure to it: "congestion of heart, lungs and kidneys; low blood pressure; muscle spasms; weight loss; damage to adrenal glands." Long-term exposure can cause cancer. Thousands of wells in America are contaminated with atrazine.

Atrazine is banned in Switzerland, which is where Syngenta is based.

---

*Growing scientific evidence suggests that the toxic chemicals we are using to grow food* are *destroying us.*

---

Fortunately, the EPA—under new leadership—has agreed to review the safety of atrazine. The USDA [US Department of Agriculture] has stated that banning atrazine would reduce crop production by 1 percent.

## We Are Becoming More Vulnerable

What is wrong with us? Why do we seem to care so little about our own safety, our own health, and the future of our children? Why are we willing to pay thousands of dollars for in vitro fertility treatments when we can't conceive, but not a few extra dollars for the organic foods that might help to preserve the reproductive health of our own and future generations?

Newspaper editorials and TV programs question whether or not organic foods are healthier for us or worth the extra cost, yet they *ignore* the growing concerns of doctors and scientists about the long-term impact of consuming foods treated with chemical fertilizers and pesticides. Whether or not organic foods are more nutritious (some studies have shown they are, some have shown they aren't) isn't the most important point.

The most important point is that growing scientific evidence suggests that the toxic chemicals we are using to grow food *are* destroying us.

Plant nutrition is a reflection of the ongoing degradation of our soil quality, seeds, and farming methods. The USDA and scientists elsewhere have been measuring the nutritional value of different foods for more than 50 years and have found significant nutrient declines in *all* crops in *all* regions over the past several decades. Scientists disagree on why this is happening, suggesting everything from inconsistent methods of measurement to agribusiness's relentless quest for higher yields, but the USDA to date has shown a shocking lack of interest in the problem. And government funding for nutritional research is microscopic compared to funding for other types of research.

Here is what we do know: Plants, animals, and people have immune systems. When we are in a natural environment and take good care of ourselves—eat right, exercise, sleep well, use basic hygiene techniques, feel loved and cared for, and actively take part in our communities—our immune systems are typically healthy and strong. Constant exposure to natural pests taps into our inner resilience and makes us stronger, enabling us to develop antibodies to fight external threats. But when we try to sterilize our environment (or the other extreme, let it be truly dirty) or try to exterminate a weed, an insect, or a disease, nature fights back just as we would, launching even stronger attacks. The result is viruses, diseases, and superpests that become resistant to pesticides. *The more we try to isolate ourselves and control nature, the weaker and more vulnerable we become.*

---

*There is enough evidence to know now that synthetic chemicals are destroying our health and our ability to reproduce and, thus, our ability to survive as a species.*

---

As Bill Miller, MD, chair of the Department of Family Medicine at the Lehigh Valley Health Network in Allentown, Pennsylvania, has observed, as a rule we are "overfed and under-germed."

There is so much more we can study to help illuminate the problems with chemicals. But there is enough evidence to know now that synthetic chemicals are destroying our health and our ability to reproduce and, thus, our ability to survive as a species. Agricultural chemicals have statistically and significantly been implicated in causing all sorts of cancers, behavioral problems, attention-deficit/hyperactivity disorder, autism, Parkinson's disease, reduced intelligence, infertility, miscarriage, diabetes, infant deformities, and low birth weight. And with endocrine disruptions come genital deformities, early puberty, gender "issues," and, again, diabetes and cancer. But all this research comes from the few scientists courageous enough to swim against the tide, to resist the easy funding offered by chemical and pharmaceutical companies and the pressure of their peers who rely on that funding.

We are allowing a few major global corporations, in collusion with our government, to poison us along with the bugs, the fungi, the weeds, and the increasingly common crop diseases. While these products are advertised as ways to control nature and our environment, we are in fact more out of control and vulnerable than ever. In our efforts to exterminate weeds, bacteria, fungi, insects, and diseases we may also be exterminating ourselves.

I am not accusing these companies of *willfully* exterminating the entire human race. That would be genocide. . . .

Much as tobacco companies suppressed information and test results that showed how deadly their products were, much as they lobbied and advertised intensively to defend their right to sell products that would kill people, the chemical companies have worked hard to quash research that suggests their products are harmful. And part of their defense has been a major advertising and lobbying push that insists we simply cannot survive without their products, without GMOs [genetically modified organisms], without chemicals. We can't feed the world without synthetic-chemical farming, they tell us.

The bad news is that China, the land that has brought us tainted toys and melamine in baby formula, is just getting on the GMO bandwagon.

> We need to begin looking at nature and this land and the soil as our allies rather than our enemies.

From the beginning of time, we've had a love/hate relationship with nature. On one hand, nature is the source of all abundance and the resources that allow us to live and thrive— all our food, our shelter, and our enjoyment. On the other hand, nature can be brutal and cruel—earthquakes, floods, droughts, and fires have often come without warning or reason. Without protection, we are vulnerable and fearful. As a species, we remember starvation, famine, and plagues and don't want those things to happen again.

What is the antidote to fear? Control. Our use of chemicals to help us grow food stems from the primal desire to control nature and plays into our fear that we won't have enough or be safe until we control nature.

Yet, it's very obvious that we will never be able to control nature. We may be able to understand it and work with it, but the universe is much larger and more powerful than any one of us or even all of us can be. The sad truth is that we are just a small blip on the surface of time, a ripple on the ocean of life. None of which has stopped us from trying to control nature, or from trying to make ourselves immortal. (And it turns out that trying to control nature can be a very lucrative business.)

We need to begin looking at nature and this land and the soil as our allies rather than our enemies. We need to be courageous enough to change the economic and political models that reward destruction. Each and every one of us needs to be willing to take action.

The results of this great chemical experiment are in and the findings are clear, yet they have been withheld, intentionally buried or, even worse, simply ignored.

Eliminating chemicals one at a time will never make a big enough difference. The chemical industry is adept at changing names and formulas just enough to placate government regulators. By seemingly eliminating known toxins like DDT, Alar (daminozide), and lead, we are lulled into an illusion of safety. But it *is* an illusion. There is only one way to ensure our safety:

We must stop poisoning ourselves now. We must remove chemicals from the process of growing, harvesting, and preserving food.

I believe it's possible to make this essential change. When you see what it's like to be a chemical farmer these days, and just how and why we ended up in this horrible situation, you will understand that it's our moral and ethical duty to change. And the possibility for success is backed by science, government studies, and frankly, common sense.

We must demand organic; and we must do it now.

# 4

# Pesticides Used on Foods Are Linked to Many Childhood Ailments

*Kelly Dorfman*

*Kelly Dorfman lectures on diet and health and has written dozens of articles on children and nutrition.*

*The chemicals now used as pesticides on our food supply were originally developed to target the nervous systems of human enemies during World War II. There is no safe level of these chemicals, especially for children. While an immediate reaction in a child may be obvious—such as a rash or upset stomach—there isn't enough information about the cumulative effect of these toxins over time. Current research suggests pesticides may be responsible for developmental delays and attention disorders as well as other behavioral health issues. Other studies link pesticide consumption to an increased risk of cancer. The best course of action one can take to safeguard their health is to avoid as much pesticide exposure as possible.*

Over the past few years, we've been hearing and reading more and more about the benefits of "eating organic," especially for pregnant women and our children. According to the Organic Trade Association, Americans spent $28 billion on organic food in 2008, which is an increase of almost $27 billion from 1990 and indicates a dramatic shift in consumers' belief in organic foods as a healthier alternative to conventionally grown or raised foods. And despite these tough economic times, demand is projected to increase even further.

Is it important to choose organic food for growing children? How bad can a few sprayed grapes and apples really be? And if they are harmful, why isn't the Food and Drug Administration [FDA] or Environmental Protection Agency (EPA) controlling the danger? The answers are simple: yes, pretty bad, and it's complicated. . . .

## Poison on Our Plants

If a child is having a direct reaction to something sprayed on his food, the symptoms usually look like some type of allergic reaction. There can be rashes, stomachaches, throat itching, or crankiness. But should you be concerned if there are no direct reactions? Yes, because not getting sick immediately is too low a standard to set for food safety. We don't know enough about what will happen down the line. Current research has shown significant ties of pesticides to triggering developmental delays. But since we cannot predict all the small or large effects caused by these poisons, I suggest we err on the side of caution.

*At some unknown point of concentration (and it's likely different for everyone), these poisons start causing subtle sensory and behavior disturbances, lack of coordination, and depressed motor function.*

Pesticides, like so many inventions, were developed by accident. Nobody set out specifically to find better ways to kill bugs on crops. Instead, scientists were looking for better ways to kill people, specifically our enemies during World War II [1939–1945]. Chemistry had advanced enough for our intrepid researchers to develop effective nerve poisons, and they did so in quantity.

Luckily, the war ended before we could use all of the poison we had developed. Consequently, by the end of the 1940s, we had warehouses full of the stuff. Rather than waste in peacetime everything they created, the chemists reconfigured the compounds in much lower doses so they could be used to kill insects and other pests. (*Pesticide* is a general term used to refer to any substance, biological agent, or device used to kill any type of rodent, microbe, or pathogens. *Insecticides* specifically target insects.) But these commercial insecticides and pesticides were originally meant as human-icides and are still toxic to people. However, because the doses are so small, it is difficult to clearly associate exposure to a specific compound with resulting symptoms.

Organophosphates, one of the most common types of insecticides, work by inhibiting cholinesterase in the nervous system. Cholinesterase is an enzyme that controls the neurotransmitter acetylcholine, which operates in the spaces between the nerve cells. By disrupting acetylcholine, high exposure to organophosphates interferes with the part of the nervous system that runs the muscles. The result is muscle twitching and depressed motor control, including breathing. Imagine the teenage monster movie where the cute girl or doomed best friend gets bitten by the alien-possessed boyfriend, starts twitching, curls up in a fetal position, and expires, and you get the general idea.

## Long-Term Effects

Of course, this does not happen if you eat, say, a conventionally raised peach without washing it. Usually what happens is absolutely nothing other than you really enjoy it—or perhaps find it a little mealy, if it's from a bad crop. And this is exactly the problem. Most of us can handle small amounts of toxins without a noticeable ill effect, but at some unknown point of concentration (and it's likely different for everyone), these poisons start causing subtle sensory and behavior disturbances, lack of coordination, and depressed motor function.

Might pesticide consumption account for why so many children have attention, health, and other behavioral issues? It is impossible to say or prove, but emerging studies are raising disturbing questions. The medical journal *Pediatrics* recently published a study looking at a link between attention-deficit hyperactivity disorder (ADHD) and exposure to organophosphate pesticides. Pesticides break down into chemicals that scientists can measure in the urine. Studying urine samples from more than a thousand children, they found that higher pesticide residues increased the chances of the child having ADHD. A California Department of Public Health study published in the journal *Environmental Health Perspectives* found that women living near fields sprayed with organochlorine pesticides (a close relative of organophosphorus pesticides) were more likely to give birth to children with autism spectrum disorders. Another study in that journal found that children who substituted organic fruits and vegetables for their conventionally grown counterparts had lower amounts of organophosphorus pesticides in their urine.

*We have very little information about what smaller exposures to various poisons do over a long period of time.*

In 2000, a National Academy of Sciences study "suggested that one out of four developmental and behavioral problems in children may be linked to genetic and environmental factors including exposure to lead, mercury, and organophosphate pesticides." Then there are the studies that found a statistical increase in cancer risk related to amount and type of pesticide exposure. Taken all together, it is enough to make any parent nervous. It also raises the question of why we aren't doing more as a country to reduce pesticide use or at least understand the risks better.

According to Dr. Michael Firestone, a senior scientist and expert on children's environmental health at the EPA, we are trying. Since 2000, the EPA in conjunction with the National Institute of Environmental Health Services has jointly funded several children's research centers to look at the effect of environmental issues on children's health. A large-scale national children's study, conducted by the National Institutes of Health and other organizations, looking at pesticides and hormone disruptors is also in the planning stages, but these projects are extremely complicated and expensive. As Dr. Firestone tactfully explains, "You cannot do direct testing on children." In other words, you cannot dose kids up with a particular pesticide and see if they get mean or stop reading or fall ill.

Instead, you can use epidemiological data, look for associations, and calculate percentage risk. Epidemiological data is information gathered from studying patterns of sickness and health in specific populations. It is used by public health officials to identify risk factors and causes of disease so that effective prevention and treatment strategies can be developed. Much epidemiological data about pesticide use is amassed because of the misfortune of people who have been accidentally acutely poisoned. Underpaid migrant farmers or factory workers are often the unwitting subjects of these studies. Although undoubtedly many of them have gotten sick from pesticide exposure, this observation does not help as much as you might think. Most people are not handling pesticides all day, so applying the disturbing findings to a more general population does not work. We have very little information about what smaller exposures to various poisons do over a long period of time.

For example, one very disturbing epidemiological study tested the blood from the umbilical cords of newborn babies from five states between December 2007 and June 2008. The researchers were looking for the presence of industrial chemicals, pesticides, and pollutants. The result found 232 potentially toxic chemicals already in their blood the day they were born. Frightening to be sure, but what does it mean? If two of those children develop autism, will it be because of one of those chemicals? Which chemical is the biggest problem? Or is it a combination of chemicals? The point of the data collection was likely to demonstrate that the next generation may be in danger because of their absorption of too many chemicals from the environment. Like much epidemiological data, it proves nothing specifically, but it does raise general concerns. Could these chemicals be causing higher cancer, autism, and/or allergy rates in this generation of children?

## Avoiding Pesticides

"We should try to reduce pesticide intake as much as possible," Dr. Firestone allows, "but it is complicated."

Aren't there standards and rules for pesticide use and residue? Of course there are, but the level of monitoring for compliance is suspect. A lawyer specializing in FDA regulations compliance whom I met at a meeting confided that because of budget restrictions, monitoring depends on the "squeal" program. In other words, your competitors squeal on you to the FDA if you are not behaving, acting like a large unpaid policing unit. The budget for monitoring compliance is "minuscule," Dr. Firestone confirms. "For example," he continues, "what fruit or vegetable do children eat the most?"

That is easy: apples, if you are counting applesauce and juice. He concurs, and I am still in the running for food *Jeopardy!*, but I sense a trick question coming up.

"Where do most apples in this country come from?" he continues.

"Washington State?" I reply tentatively.

"China," he sighs. "The land of things that never get tested."

In fact, according to a CNN report, 50 percent of the apple juice imported to the United States comes from China.

The U.S. Apple Association claims that 47 percent of all the apples on the planet come from China.

The bottom line? It just seems to make logical sense to avoid as many toxins as you reasonably can, even though it may not yet be possible to link symptoms directly to pesticides.

# 5

# Organic Food Still Contains Pesticides

*Joanne Levasseur and Vera-Lynn Kubinec*

*Joanne Levasseur and Vera-Lynn Kubinec are journalists with the Canadian Broadcasting Corporation (CBC).*

*Organic foods tested by the Canadian Food Inspection Agency showed that nearly half contained pesticides not allowed in organic food production. Although some producers may be intentionally using the banned chemicals, in most cases it's more likely that the produce was contaminated by drift from neighboring farms or contaminated soil or water. Although none of the tests showed unsafe levels, there is room for improvement in organic food production to ensure that products labeled organic are not contaminated with pesticides.*

Nearly half the organic fresh fruits and vegetables tested across Canada in the past two years contained pesticide residue, according to a CBC News analysis of data supplied by the Canadian Food Inspection Agency (CFIA).

Of the 45.8 per cent of samples that tested positive for some trace of pesticide, a smaller amount—1.8 per cent—violated Canada's maximum allowable limits for the presence of pesticides, the data shows.

The data released to CBC News under the federal Access to Information Act includes testing of organic fruits and vegetables sampled between September 2011 and September 2013.

The results were not what Winnipeg organic consumer Mathieu Rey was expecting.

"I would hope that the products are without pesticides. That is what I would be looking for," Rey said in an interview.

"I'm trusting the companies to provide a non-pesticide or pesticide-free product."

As widespread as the pesticide residues were, they were still considerably less than the 78.4 per cent of non-organic samples the inspection agency found containing pesticide residues, violating the allowable limits 4.7 per cent of the time.

The CFIA told CBC News that none of the test results posed a health risk. The agency did not prevent any of the food from being sold as organic.

---

*We see pesticide residues throughout our environment. . . . So unfortunately, it's really hard to have a zero pesticide residue any longer.*

---

## Organic Trade Group Concerned

Most of the fresh produce sampled was imported, with only one-fifth of it grown in Canada.

Of the domestically grown samples, about 43 per cent tested positive for at least one pesticide—slightly lower than the 46 per cent of imported samples.

Matthew Holmes, executive director of the Ottawa-based Canada Organic Trade Association, called the findings concerning.

"We see pesticide residues throughout our environment. It's in our soil, they're in our water, drinking water now, and there's new reports coming out showing there's pesticides in fetal cord blood. So unfortunately, it's really hard to have a zero pesticide residue any longer," he said.

Pesticides were measured in amounts as little as 0.0001 parts per million (ppm) to greater than three ppm.

"These are very low amounts," Holmes said.

Rick Holley, an expert in food safety at the University of Manitoba, agreed the residue measurements are small.

But Holley added that the data indicate that consumers who often pay extra to buy organic food might not always be getting their money's worth.

"If the money is being spent to avoid pesticide residues and have access to food which is healthy, then I think the money is not well-spent," he said. "[Pesticides] will not be absent."

Holley said that's partly because the analytical methodologies are capable of detecting residues in parts per billion or parts per trillion, well below the allowable limits.

## How Pesticides Get on Organic Produce

He explained that pesticides can get onto organic produce through contamination of water or soil through pesticide spray drift from neighbouring farms, and through contact with non-organic produce after harvest.

But Holley said some of the larger residue measurements suggest an organic producer deliberately used a pesticide that is not allowed.

"Where pesticide residue levels are at or above the maximum residue levels prescribed, then I think that there's probably reasonable evidence that that has been the situation," he said.

Take, for example, an organic tomato imported from Mexico, sampled in the Manitoba-Saskatchewan region. It was tested for four different pesticides and contained residues of two of them—both in amounts that exceeded the allowable limits for those pesticides.

In contrast, some of the samples tested positive for numerous pesticides but at lower levels.

An organic pepper imported from Mexico and sampled in Quebec was analyzed for 13 different pesticides and was found to contain minute amounts of 10 of them.

None of the amounts measured on that pepper violated the maximum allowable residue limits for the pesticides in question.

Holmes said past studies have shown the quantity and incidence of pesticide residues in organic produce are consistently lower than those in non-organic.

Analysis of the fungicide thiabendazole in the CFIA's latest data suggests the amount of pesticide present in the organic produce is lower than on regular produce.

The average quantity of thiabendazole measured on organic apples was 0.02 ppm whereas the average amount measured on non-organic was 0.3 ppm—about 15 times higher.

---

*Synthetic pesticides are not allowed under certified organic production regulations, but some other types of pesticides are permitted.*

---

"I think consumers are looking for not necessarily a zero level, but they're looking to not contribute to the pesticide residues that are out there and they're looking to reduce their exposure as much as possible. And I still think we're seeing in this data that organic offers that," Holmes said.

He acknowledged there is room for improvement on the part of organic producers, and said he would like to see the amount of pesticide as low as possible.

"The organic sector absolutely believes in continuous improvement, and I would love to see that level go down for all products, not just organic," said Holmes.

Synthetic pesticides are not allowed under certified organic production regulations, but some other types of pesticides are permitted.

The CFIA did not analyze the data to determine what proportion of the positive tests are for pesticides permitted in organic production.

Some types of organic produce had a higher rate of residue presence than others. For example, 77 per cent of organic grape samples tested positive; apples were in the middle at 45 per cent testing positive; carrots had a lower positive rate at 30 per cent.

## Organics Remain Better

Mark Kastel, a farm policy analyst at the Cornucopia Institute in Wisconsin, said even with nearly half the organic samples containing pesticide residues, organics are still better than non-organic produce.

"It's a dramatically lower figure than conventional food, so it illustrates the advantages of organics. But it's also very disturbing that it very clearly illustrates the fact that we've soiled our own bed," Kastel said in an interview with CBC News from his farm near Rockton, Wis.

"Since 1950, we've seen an exponential increase in the use of synthetic toxic chemicals to grow our food, and that there now is a high level of contamination in the soil, in groundwater, in surface water," he added.

"Obviously we're concerned in the organic industry about fraud," said Kastel, who has been both an advocate and watchdog of the organic industry on both sides of the Canada-U.S. border.

"I'm very comfortable that the vast majority of all organic fruits and vegetables and other commodities are produced with high integrity, but we do need to protect the ethical farmers that are participating, and businesses in the organic industry—and, most importantly, consumers who are seeking authentic food."

Kastel called on government regulators to do a better job of scrutinizing organic produce.

The Canadian government brought in the Organic Products Regulations in 2009 requiring organic food producers to have their products certified by an accredited third-party certification body.

The certifiers conduct annual farm and facility inspections meant to ensure the organic producers are following the rules.

Rola Yehia, acting national manager of the CFIA's consumer protection division, said, "If there is non-permitted substances found in organic products, we would notify the CFIA-accredited certification body who would request the organic operator to take corrective action."

"So we have the system in place, and we have the confidence in our system, and we have the mechanism to address any non-compliances if they arise," said Yehia, whose oversight includes the Canada Organic Office of the CFIA.

"We have a good relationship with the industry, so we work together to correct any gaps in the system," Yehia added.

Despite the presence of pesticide residues, consumer Mathieu Rey said he will continue to buy organic.

"That would encourage me to get to know local farmers more and more, get to know the community-supported agriculture in each neighbourhood," he said, adding that he thinks that's the best way to know what's in the food he buys.

6

# Organic Food Is Nutritionally Superior

*Erin Smith, Charles Benbrook, and Donald R. Davis*

*Erin Smith is a policy director with the Pennsylvania Department of Agriculture. Charles Benbrook is research professor at the Center for Sustaining Agriculture and Natural Resources at Washington State University at Puyallup. Donald R. Davis is research associate at Washington State University at Pullman.*

*At least 60 percent of organic produce contains more nutrients than conventionally grown produce. One reason for this may be that organic plants are able to create more robust root systems in the soil for the absorption of nutrients. Organic grains also contain higher levels of antioxidants due to the increased need for the plant to create photochemicals, many of which have antioxidant properties in humans. More research is needed to ensure that organic farms can create high yields without losing these benefits.*

In the Center's [The Organic Center] 2008 report, *New Evidence Confirms the Nutritional Superiority of Plant-Based Organic Foods*, we presented research demonstrating that organically grown crops, including grains, have on average higher nutrient contents than those grown conventionally. Many variables influence nutrient content, often making it difficult to determine the impact of farming systems on nutrient levels.

Thus there are conflicting results about this issue, with some studies finding significant differences in organic crops, others showing little or no differences, and those that report—for a few nutrients—conventionally grown food with higher levels.

## Study Findings

Matched-pair studies are the best way to control for these variables and to isolate their influences on nutrient content. For the 2008 report, The Organic Center developed a rigorous methodology to screen research studies comparing the nutrient content of organic and conventional crops. We identified 191 matched-pair studies that met our criteria designed to limit the influence of extraneous environmental and genetic factors on nutrients. These criteria required studies to use the same plant varieties in the same location during the same year. Out of these matched pairs, 62% of the organic samples, including fruits, vegetables and a few grains, had higher nutrient levels. Conventional systems had higher nutrient levels in 36% of the matched pairs. The average serving of organic plant-based food contained about 25% more of the nutrients encompassed in this study than a comparable-sized serving of the same food produced by conventional farming methods. The full report can be read at www.organic-center.org/reportfiles/NutrientContentReport.pdf.

---

*One of the greatest nutrient differences found between organic and non-organic grain is antioxidant content.*

---

Whereas most of the research conducted five or ten years ago focused on fruits and vegetables, there is now more research on organic grains. These studies support the superiority of organic grains regarding some nutrients, especially antioxidants. The differences between organic and conventional grains tend to be less than those found in fruits and vegetables. But overall, there is agreement that consistent differences do exist, especially in antioxidant levels. This trend makes sense in light of the effects of conventional high-yield farming methods. . . . Without chemical fertilizers and other inputs, grains grown organically are able to produce healthy roots and develop a more robust array of phytochemicals and micronutrients.

At the Organic World Congress in 2008, [K.] Murphy et al. presented a report on 35 different varieties of soft white wheat grown in side-by-side organic and conventional farming systems in Washington state. The organic crops were significantly higher in copper, magnesium, manganese, zinc and phosphorus. Only calcium was higher in conventionally grown grain. There was no difference found in iron content. Most of these minerals were not higher in the organic soil. In fact, copper, manganese, and zinc had lower concentrations in the organic soil. Only phosphorus had a greater concentration in both the soil and the grain.

Researchers suggest that mycorrhizal fungi present in organic fields from the application of organic matter may result in increased uptake of soil nutrients and higher concentration in wheat. Genetics still plays an important role; even in organic systems the concentrations of many micronutrients and antioxidants still vary among varieties. Murphy et al. found significant difference in nutrient content between cultivars, particularly for calcium, copper, magnesium, manganese, and phosphorus. This led the researchers to conclude, "certain cultivars may be optimally adapted to organic farming systems in a way that allows for higher grain mineral concentration. These cultivars are likely capable of exploiting the higher organic matter in the organic systems to achieve higher nutritional value".

## Antioxidants

One of the greatest nutrient differences found between organic and non-organic grain is antioxidant content. With fewer inputs, such as synthetic pesticides and fertilizers, organic farming systems tend to mimic natural stress conditions. This encourages plants to produce a broader array of phytochemicals for protection from these stresses. Most of these phytochemicals have antioxidant activity in humans.

Whole grains are particularly high in phenolic compounds, tocopherols, and carotenoids. These and other phytochemicals occur in plants in two forms—free/soluble and bound/insoluble. Free forms of phytochemicals dissolve quickly and are immediately absorbed into the bloodstream. Bound forms are attached to the wall of plant cells and must be released by intestinal bacteria during digestion before being absorbed. Bound forms are predominant in grains, but most research has measured only free forms. As such the antioxidant content of grains is often underestimated.

---

*As yields increase, organic crops, including wheat and other grains, are at risk of losing this nutrient advantage.*

---

In a 2003 study, [K.K.] Adom et al. found that bound antioxidant compounds in wheat were as much as 17-fold higher than free antioxidant compounds. Interestingly, because most of the antioxidant activity in grains is released in the colon, this may partly explain the association between increased consumption of wheat and other whole grains and reduced incidence of gastrointestinal diseases.

In a forthcoming report, we will discuss in depth the difference in antioxidant content of organic and non-organic grains.

Organic grain is still susceptible to the dilution effect. As demand for organic grain increases, there is pressure for plant scientists to produce organic crops with higher yields. As yields increase, organic crops, including wheat and other grains, are at risk of losing this nutrient advantage. Some researchers hope that plant breeding that emphasizes both nutrient content and yield will minimize dilution effects in organic crops. Others believe that organic farming can already match conventional yields and maintain nutrient content if farmers continue to encourage healthy soils rich in organic matter and properly select varieties with both high yields and high concentrations of nutrients. In fact, according to some researchers, organic farming—at least in the developing world—is the only method that has been able to improve both yield and nutritional quality at the same time. This is an important field of continued research.

# 7

# Organic Foods Are Not Better than Conventionally Grown Foods

*Morgan Bahl*

*At the time of this writing, Morgan Bahl was a student at Iowa State University.*

*When it comes to health, there is no difference between organic and conventional produce. Both offer the same nutrient benefits. While choosing to eat fresh produce is better for your health than processed food, choosing organic does not lead to any additional benefits. This is good news for those trying to manage a tight budget.*

You may have noticed when you walk into the produce department at the local Hy-Vee there are fruits and vegetables with the label "ORGANIC" plastered all over their packaging and displays, often accompanied with head-scratching prices.

Do you get what you pay for? Are organic foods actually better for your health? Should we all be eating organic or is it a fad, money-making marketing scheme? What even makes a food "organic?"

There are lots of questions you might ask yourself before paying such high prices. Unfortunately, the food industry is misleading consumers on this topic and using the lure of health claims to make extra profit.

"Normal" foods are healthy, nutritious and safe just as they are, which makes organic foods an unnecessary product choice. This is good news for many college students because they are also budget busters and we all know that none of us have the money for that.

## The Organic Label

So what makes a food item organic? The USDA [US Department of Agriculture] defines organic foods as ones that preserve biodiversity, support animal health and welfare, use approved materials, are inspected on site and utilize fewer herbicides and pesticides. These foods undergo inspections and require farmers to be certified as organic growers, a long process that requires high levels of commitment.

When consumers hear the term "organic," many expect foods that are treated with fewer or no "bad chemicals," foods that are more nutritious, or "natural," and those that are less processed or may entail closer care and attention to crops and livestock. However, this is a long list of expectations that are difficult to meet, so the question is actually whether or not the certification process and benefits are worth the hassle.

---

*[Food designated] "100% organic" is given the USDA seal and shows that the product was raised separately, is not a genetically modified organism, and contains only organic ingredients.*

---

Becoming certified is a process that many farmers choose not to go through because of the time commitment and the specific standards. USDA certification requires a 3-year documented history of the farm procedures and practices. Qualifying farmers have to plan their use of organic seeds, pest control aids, manure and composting, while also preventing crop contact with non-organic substances by means of drift, harvest and shipping.

Rose Martin, senior lecturer in food science and human nutrition at Iowa State [University], often discusses this topic and reassures others that, due to this intensive process, we can feel confident that if we choose to buy organic foods, we will be getting foods that meet the USDA federal regulations for organic growing.

Given that the food meets regulations, it can be labelled as either "100% organic", "organic" or "made with organic ingredients," as regulated by the National Organic Standards Board.

"100% organic" is given the USDA seal and shows that the product was raised separately, is not a genetically modified organism, and contains only organic ingredients. The label "organic" is also able to display the [USDA] seal but is made with at least 95% organic ingredients.

The "made with organic ingredients" label indicates at least 70% organic ingredients but cannot display the USDA's seal on its packaging. A point to remember with organic certification and labeling is that they give no indication of food safety or nutrition.

When consumers see the USDA stamp of approval, the foods are often given a "health halo" and are regarded as more beneficial than conventionally grown foods, but they do not necessarily deserve that reputation.

According to Martin, "nutritionally, there is no significant difference between organic and conventionally grown foods." Both are nutritionally adequate and thus there is no additional health benefit for choosing organic foods.

One of the biggest health interests associated with organic foods is the reduced use of chemicals or use of so-called natural chemicals. While it is true that organic foods have less pesticide residue than conventional products, the benefit is negligible.

The pesticide residue found on non-organic foods is so low that consumers are taking in less than 5 percent of the Acceptable Dietary Intake.

This means that when we eat most non-organic foods, we are taking in 95 percent less than the amount we are able to ingest and be completely safe from harm. This is enough to put pesticide concerns to rest and show that the lowered presence of chemicals on organic foods is essentially meaningless.

The perceived "benefit" of lower pesticides is countered with the high prices. Because of the more labor-intensive process and the lower product yields, the prices can be very expensive, up to 50–100% higher than conventional foods.

With all factors weighed, choosing organic foods is unnecessary for good health and nutrition. Martin summarized this debate well by saying that, "We cannot say that organic is better, but food is better . . . broccoli is better."

Really, eating healthy is about making the case for good food choices. Choose fruits and vegetables which are nutritious and protective, regardless of their processing methods.

Luckily, there is no "right or wrong" decision between organic and non-organic foods and it comes down to your preferences. There's nothing wrong with them, but there is also not necessarily anything significantly special about them.

If you wish to pay $6.00 for that bag of oranges, that is fine, but rest easy knowing that if you choose non-organic foods instead, you are not doing your body any disfavors or compromising your health.

# 8

# Science Doesn't Support Organic Food Claims

*Dennis Myers*

*Dennis Myers is a writer with the* Reno News and Review.

*While the safety of genetically modified organisms (GMOs) are debated by the public, the scientific community has widely accepted them as both safe and necessary. Opponents contend that GMOs are dangerous for human health and that products containing GMO ingredients should be labeled as such. However, even organic farmers use some synthetic pesticides and plants themselves create toxins to deter insects. Further, genetically altered food helped the world population avoid famine in the past and could be more useful if opponents didn't block its use.*

The crowd stretched entirely around the front of the downtown Reno [Nevada] federal building.

Protest signs attacked transgenic food. "Your food—brought to you by the makers of AGENT ORANGE." "It's a SAD day when 'NORMAL' food is hard to find!" "HELL NO GMOS." There were also angrier signs attacking [agricultural biotechnology company] Monsanto, and for other causes—Native American, veterans, the National Defense Authorization Act.

It would have been easy to assume this was a group of flat earthers, and I suspect they were being characterized that way by plenty of observers on this day of coast-to-coast anti-transgenic food protests. But I knew some of these people as smart and sensible. Like a lot of science-oriented people, I didn't understand why some of them were present. This was another sortie in what scientists have begun calling "The Liberal War on Science."

Many in this crowd cite the fact that there's no known instance in history of death caused by marijuana but endless deaths caused by booze and tobacco. But they reject the fact that no one is known to have ever died from transgenic foods but plenty of people in history have died from natural, organic foods through salmonella, E. coli., etc. "Transgenic" is the scientific term for what activists call genetically modified food or organisms—GMOs.

Many of those present are frustrated by the refusal of climate change critics to accept the findings of a scientific panel that has examined all the science and found that climate change is real and mostly caused by human activity. But most of them ignore the findings of a similar panel that upheld the safety and usefulness of transgenic foods.

## GMOs and the Scientific Community

Grant Cramer is a biochemist at the University of Nevada, Reno. He began his work on the campus studying cold tolerance of plants. At some point he got into grapes. "Some years we've had a little trouble because it's cold, but for most years we've grown them and made grapes and made wine from them," he said. "That's the feasible part. Then, with time, we've started to realize that we were giving them too much water. That was part of the problem. So we started reducing the water and found out that . . . we can get by with 12 times less water and produce better quality grapes than alfalfa requires. So from a point of view of using our water wisely in a state where water is a critical issue, it's an ideal crop to grow."

Now he consults with Nevada vineyards to help them with their crops. It's a small contribution to economic development in Nevada. He doesn't use genetic modification.

---

*We've been genetically modifying plants for 10,000 years, from the very first farmers who selected.*

---

"In my laboratory we can genetically modify plants," he said. "We don't do it, for the most part. Sometimes we do it just to understand the function of a gene. But our goal is not to go out there and create a new grape."

But he doesn't want modification removed from his tool chest, either, pointing out that while there are now new procedures for doing it, the practice itself goes back centuries.

"We've been genetically modifying plants for 10,000 years, from the very first farmers who selected. If you go and look at the old wild corn, the Native Americans were selecting for bigger and bigger cobs. So they were modifying or crossing plants. We've done that with every crop we have today."

Some wine purists are not crazy about fiddling with grapes. "That may change in the future when they get a disease that is a problem," Cramer said.

That, in fact, was what happened with the papaya. For a long time, Papaya ringspot virus (PRSV), was minor in its impact. Then it began to mutate into a much more damaging form. During the late 20th century the industry was nearly wiped out. Science came to the rescue. Transgenic PRSV-resistant varieties were developed. The industry is back.

The new technology, according to Cramer, allows the process to be better controlled by scientists, making it better than cross breeding in the field.

"If anything, breeding is much more dangerous than genetic engineering. You're crossing thousands upon thousands of genes with another species or organisms and you don't know what you're going to get out of that. You could be producing some new compounds in that new plant. . . . You didn't know if you had an allergy for it, you didn't know if it had this or that. Nowadays, everything's tested, tested, tested, tested."

All of this is basic in the scientific community. The only places it's being debated are outside that community. Scientists have moved on.

## Objections to Transgenic Food

I wanted to find out what motivated folks who are supporters of science to reject transgenic foods, so I called one I saw at the federal building protest. Jan Gilbert is very smart and tough—a skillful, knowledgeable lobbyist until retiring a couple of years ago. The White House website calls her a "Champion of Change." She told me she went to the protest in part to support a friend who is an anti-transgenic activist.

"I went in some ways to support her and the work she is doing," Gilbert said. "I think there are some real problems with modified food, and I think we need to have them labeled. That was the main point of that rally, and I don't think that's a difficult thing to do. I just think it's a matter of information, that we should know what we're buying."

I get the part about supporting a friend. Relying on allies is basic to politics.

Gilbert emphasized the information issue. There have been efforts to require labeling of transgenic foods in legislatures—Assembly Bill 330 at last year's [2013] Nevada Legislature—though the motives of the movement are not exactly pure. It wants labeling in order to stigmatize transgenics, and cherry-picks the modified foods it wants included—only foods modified by certain procedures, not *all* modified foods. This goes back to its claim that there's a difference between foods modified in the field and in the lab. Nevertheless, there is a case to be made for labeling.

"Monsanto and the grocers are just paying millions of dollars to keep it from happening, so you have to wonder why they won't do it to have this information in our homes," Gilbert said.

---

*I suspect trust has a lot to do with the problems transgenic foods have.*

---

Indeed, there really is no reason not to have labeling, and it's in the interest of the corporations. If they simply started doing the labeling themselves, and included all modified foods, not just lab-modified, the public would quickly understand that *most* of the food we already eat has been genetically modified.

Gilbert is also suspicious of corporate money that can taint studies of the safety of transgenics. "The subsidies of scientific studies can be compromising," she said.

I suspect trust has a lot to do with the problems transgenic foods have. It requires trust in science and scientists, the kind of trust the nation had in the eras of vaccine discoveries. Today, however, we are in an age when trust is not easy to come by, particularly trust in large institutions. To the events of the last half century that fundamentally undermined public faith—U-2 [1960], Vietnam [War 1959–1975], Watergate [1972], Iran-Contra [1986], WMDs [weapons of mass destruction]—must be added the ability of the corporate community and malefactors of great wealth to pay skilled opinion manipulators to employ public relations techniques that make falsehood and deception credible, as in the case of climate change.

Monsanto is a gigantic entity, and an arrogant one. Its lobbying and use of patent law and abuse of farmers is hard to get down. Moreover, the industry has had its own scandals. Archer Daniels Midland [ADM] was involved in scandals bigger than Watergate in the 1990s, but news of its activities was deemphasized on both commercial and public television that took ADM money—making journalism harder to trust.

No state knows better than Nevada how difficult trust in science can be. The Atomic Energy Commission's rent-a-scientist assured the state of the safety of Nevada nuclear testing when they knew otherwise. Gilbert knows that history.

## Food Safety

When Athens [Greece] executed [philosopher] Socrates, it gave him natural, organic food—hemlock.

Some 2,400 years later, American Spirit markets its cigarettes with slogans like "made with organic tobacco grown on American soil" and "Natural tastes better."

---

*While some critics call pesticides unnatural, that's hard to support in view of the fact that plants themselves produce pesticides—and that organic farmers use pesticides.*

---

There's nothing magic about natural food. It ranges from healthy to lethal. There *is* something magic about genetically engineered food. So far, at least, all of it is safe.

Traditional farmers use synthetic fertilizers. Organic farmers use manure. Think about that for a moment in the light of simple common sense. What would be more likely to produce pathogens—chemicals or manure? In fact, a study of produce from organic and traditional farms found E. coli five times more often in the organic samples.

As for pesticides, while some critics call pesticides unnatural, that's hard to support in view of the fact that plants themselves produce pesticides—and that organic farmers use pesticides.

"Plants produce pesticides of their own, poisons to prevent the infection from attacking," Cramer said. "So when an insect starts chewing on the leaf, it tells the plant it's under attack. What does it do? It starts producing more of the poison. So a plant that's attacked by insects is more poisonous than a plant that's not attacked by insects. So what they did was a study of a comparison of the poisonous chemicals in the non-transgenic normal corn with the transgenic and they found out that the transgenic corn produced less of the poisonous chemicals to defend itself than the non-transgenic. . . . So in fact, the transgenic corn was healthier for a human."

Both traditional and organic farmers use pesticides, but those used by organic farmers can be health risks. Organic pesticides are produced from natural sources with less processing. Biologist Christie Wilcox wrote in *Scientific American* that it "turns out that there are over 20 chemicals commonly used in the growing and processing of organic crops that are approved by the US Organic Standards. . . . [M]any organic pesticides that are also used by conventional farmers are used more intensively than synthetic ones due to their lower levels of effectiveness. According to the National Center for Food and Agricultural Policy, the top two organic fungicides, copper and sulfur, were used at a rate of 4 and 34 pounds per acre in 1971. In contrast, the synthetic fungicides only required a rate of 1.6 lbs per acre, less than half the amount of the organic alternatives."

Some natural pesticides are health risks. One of them, Rotonone, is so toxic that it was taken off the market for a time. It was Rotonone that the state of California used in its 1997 effort to poison the unwanted northern pike in Davis Lake 55 miles northwest of Reno.

As for nutrition, first of all, it's kind of a so-what issue. People in the United States are not short on nutrients. But for those concerned about it, here it is:

In 2012, a study was released of the available research on nutrition in foods. A team of Stanford [University] researchers examined 17 studies of the effect of organic and non-organic grown foods on humans and 223 other studies solely of the nutritional and contaminant contents of foods. This was not a contest of organics versus transgenics, or even of processed foods. Rather, it examined nutrient and contaminant content based on how the foods (meat and eggs, fruits and vegetables, etc.) were grown—organically grown food compared to traditionally grown food.

In a prepared statement, senior author of the final report Dena Bravata said, "There isn't much difference between organic and conventional foods, if you're an adult and making a decision based solely on your health." The team "did not find strong evidence that organic foods are more nutritious or carry fewer health risks than conventional alternatives, though consumption of organic foods can reduce the risk of pesticide exposure," according to a Stanford release at the time the study was published in the *Annals of Internal Medicine.*

---

*One of the best bits of evidence that transgenic food is safe is that virtually everyone eats it with no ill effects. Grocery stores, after all, are loaded with it.*

---

There were findings in favor of organics. Some of the studies reviewed by the team, for instance, did find lower pesticide presence in humans, though there was no evidence of any clinical consequence to the small difference. Organic food supporters were nevertheless outraged by the findings.

A similar review by six British scientists of 12 studies found "no evidence or differences in nutrition-related health outcomes that result from exposure to organic or conventionally produced foodstuffs." It did find that organic foods were higher in fats, but not much higher.

One of the best bits of evidence that transgenic food is safe is that virtually everyone eats it with no ill effects. Grocery stores, after all, are loaded with it.

## Questionable Environmental Benefits

Organic foods benefit from the perception that they are better for the environment, but the evidence suggests otherwise. Traditional farming is very efficient and becoming more so all the time, getting more foodstuffs from each square foot of land, which can shield some land—including wilderness—from being used for farmland. Organic food accounts for only a tiny percentage of agricultural markets. If it ever became a major economic force, it could be environmentally ruinous. Most organic farming produces a fourth fewer crops on average than traditional farming, according to a study in the journal *Nature*. "Feeding the world with organic food would require vast new tracts of farmland," according to *New Yorker* science writer Michael Specter. "Without ripping out the rainforests, there just isn't enough of it left."

---

*Many organic food supporters oppose transgenic foods with a fierceness and emotion that is sometimes vicious, and has even spilled over into violence.*

---

University of California, Davis scientist Pamela Ronald goes further. Writing in the journal *Genetics*, she argues that millions of lives depend on genetically improved seed because arable land is limited, urbanization, salinization and other forms of environmental damage have ruined much land, and water supplies are under greater pressure from overpopulation and pollution. Humankind *must* get more crops from less land. "[I]t is no longer possible to simply open up more undeveloped land for cultivation to meet production needs. . . . Thus, increased food production must largely take place on the same land area while using less water." Indeed, she wrote, transgenics have been a lifesaver to the environment. "Without the development of high yielding crop varieties over recent decades, two to four times more land would have been needed in the United States, China and India to produce the same amount of food."

## Genetically Modified Food Saved the World

There was the time genetically modified food saved the world. In 1968, biologist Paul Ehrlich wrote in his book *The Population Bomb*, "In the 1970s, hundreds of millions of people will starve to death. . . . India couldn't possibly feed two hundred million more people by 1980." Food riots began in India even before the book got into print. And there was no certainty the famine would stop with the subcontinent.

But mass famine didn't happen, even in India. Why? Because science came to the rescue with genetically modified food—dwarf wheat, developed by Norman Borlaug, who received the Nobel Prize for saving huge swaths of humankind. His disease resistant wheats produced larger harvests—the "green revolution."

*Organic advocates have been chillingly effective in spreading false information about transgenic foods, with the result that those foods are stigmatized throughout Europe and Africa.*

Interestingly, scientists and other experts who support transgenic foods are almost uniformly supportive of organic foods, too. But many, many organic food supporters oppose transgenic foods with a fierceness and emotion that is sometimes vicious, and has even spilled over into violence on the edges of the movement. Transgenic critics call Borlaug's achievement a mistake. Blogger Jill Richardson called his work "unsustainable" in an essay posted on the liberal Common Dreams website. One "healthy living" website calls Borlaug's wheat "Another Arrow in the Backs of Americans."

After the Stanford study was released, Rosie Mestel of the *Los Angeles Times* reported that the reaction of transgenic critics to the study was to "start a petition to have the study retracted, and to accuse the researchers of bias and being in the pay of nefarious industry concerns."

Organic advocates have been chillingly effective in spreading false information about transgenic foods, with the result that those foods are stigmatized throughout Europe and Africa. Legal restrictions have been imposed in country after country—Kenya outlawed them outright—and what law has not done, the stigma has.

What is particularly disturbing about the hostility to transgenic foods on the left is that it hurts those who liberals normally try to help. "Every year, 500,000 children become blind as a result of vitamin A deficiency and 70 percent die within a year of losing their sight," Hoover Institution scientist Henry Miller has written, describing the maladies golden rice was created to prevent.

Golden rice was invented by German cell biologist Peter Beyer and Swiss plant biologist Ingo Potrykus. It incorporates beta-carotene, a vitamin A precursor, into rice grains. Potrykus, in a gesture akin to Jonas Salk's refusal to patent the polio vaccine, has allowed golden rice to be provided free to subsistence farmers, and it can be licensed free to developing nations. In August 2000, Monsanto announced it would give away patent rights to golden rice, a godsend to malnourished children around the world. In the Philippines, golden rice test fields have been damaged by anti-transgenic vandals.

But in part because of the stigma surrounding transgenic foods, golden rice has become bogged down in approval bureaucracy. In some countries, golden rice has taken longer in the regulatory pipeline than it took to develop in the lab (nine years).

Some advocates are fighting back. Canadian ecologist Patrick Moore, former president of Greenpeace Canada, has been holding anti-Greenpeace protests in Europe and Canada to demand that the wraps be taken off golden rice and to highlight Greenpeace's role in opposing golden rice foods. "Eight million children have died unnecessarily since golden rice was invented," he said in a prepared statement. "How many more million can Greenpeace carry on its conscience?"

But most scientists prefer to let their work speak for them, which leaves the field to critics—which is how the stigma was created in the first place.

# 9

# Synthetic Ingredients Should Not Be Allowed in Organic Food

*Jenny Hopkinson*

*Jenny Hopkinson covers agriculture and food policy issues for POLITICO Pro news service.*

*Producers of organic foods argue about which synthetic materials can be used in products that carry the organic label. Baking soda, for example, is synthetic but can be used in organic bakery goods. There are over two hundred items on the "allowable" list, including some antibiotics. Many organic advocates and consumer groups believe the products should be more pure, while some large producers argue that the demand cannot be met without the help of some synthetic ingredients.*

The organic apple in your lunch might come from a tree treated with an antibiotic. The organic milk in your coffee this morning could have come from a cow that—a little more than a year ago—could be found on a conventional farm, treated with antibiotics and fed non-organic grain. And that organic chicken in the oven? There's a chance it's been fed a synthetic amino acid.

All these things are allowed under the green and white "USDA [US Department of Agriculture] Organic" seal on packages in the grocery store, but there's a civil war raging in the industry over how much longer such exceptions should be permitted and how to best get rid of them. The antibiotic used on apple trees is already on its way out.

It's a fight that played out this week [end of April 2014] in San Antonio [Texas], where a 15-member panel charged by Congress with advising the Agriculture Department on its organic food standards haggled over a large stack of seemingly obscure rules. But while these organic food specialists were arguing over the use of streptomycin—the antibiotic used on apple trees—and methionine—the amino acid put in chicken feed—there's a much bigger implication for that coveted "USDA Organic" label.

## Popularity of Organic

Organic food and fiber sales grew to $35 billion in 2013, up 11.5 percent from 2012, and that was before recent announcements from Target and Wal-Mart that they are upping their role in the game. American consumers are increasingly looking for food that is free of pesticides, antibiotics and synthetics, leaving what was once a niche industry struggling to meet the demand for foods that are certified as organic.

"Organic is booming, and the mainstream acceptance of organic products is driving it," said Steve Crider, liaison for government and industry affairs for Amy's Kitchen, a California-based organic and natural food maker. Conventional retailers are enthusiastically stocking organic products, and demand is fast outpacing supply, thanks in large part to the interest of the coveted "millennial" consumer.

"We are coming into the second generation of organic consumers: the kids who were raised on this stuff by their moms," Crider said. "They get it about food and sustainability and organic and local. They are part of the drivers of this."

Which is why the meeting this week of the National Organic Standards Board [NOSB] was more than just an obscure food standards debate and the site of so much contention.

The start of the meeting Tuesday [April 29, 2014] was delayed for roughly an hour when a half-dozen consumer advocates blocked the panel with a sign that read "Safeguard Organics" and chanted "Don't change sunset." The event resumed after San Antonio police arrived and arrested one of the protesters.

---

*There are more than 200 synthetic, non-organic and other materials that the National Organic Program allows to be used for specific purposes in organic food products and production.*

---

At the crux of the protestors' complaints is a long-standing issue within the organic industry: the pace at which non-organic and synthetic materials should be removed from the program.

## Synthetic Ingredients Allowed Under the Organic Label

When the organic standards were first crafted in the 1990s, Congress and USDA recognized that the program would have to allow for the limited use of some non-organic materials that are deemed not to have health or environmental risks, at least initially, until alternatives could be found.

As a result, sodium bicarbonate—better known as baking soda—is permitted as a leavening agent in organic baked goods, for example. Similarly, synthetic methionine can be added to organic chicken feed to ensure the birds get the appropriate amount of amino acid.

All told, there are more than 200 synthetic, non-organic and other materials that the National Organic Program [NOP] allows to be used for specific purposes in organic food products and production. To encourage the development of organic alternatives, the program's creators crafted rules to require that such materials be re-approved every five years or "sunset" out of use.

The issue has come to a head following a September [2013] decision by USDA, made without the opportunity for public comment, to change the board's method for reviewing the way it allows for the continued use of synthetic and nonorganic materials in organic products. While all such materials will still undergo review every five years, it will now take a two-thirds vote of the board to remove each item from the list of what is accepted.

"It's a thorough and transparent review process for all substances," allowing for two public comment periods, Miles McEvoy, undersecretary of USDA's Agricultural Marketing Service and head of the NOP, explained at the San Antonio meeting in defense of the move. Overall, the change "simplifies the process," he said.

But organic watch-dog groups are vehement in their objections.

The move was little more than a "power grab on the part of the USDA," Mark Kastel, head of Cornucopia Institute, told the board. Kastel and his group—which represents many small farms and the old guard of the organic food movement—have threatened to sue the government, alleging that the change should have been subject to formal rule-making procedures.

What's more, added Lisa Bunin, organic policy director for the Center for Food Safety, the change to the rules "undermines congressional authority," removes "the incentives of continuous improvement" and "breeds complacency."

"Credibility of the organic brand and consumer markets is driven by organic integrity, not meeting the lowest common denominator," Bunin said. "Market growth based on increasing the number of synthetics in organics is a recipe for failure."

The larger organic industry, meanwhile, argues that while the ultimate goal is for organic to be as pure as possible, flexibility is needed to continue answering the growing demand of consumers.

Organic producers had petitioned the NOSB for changes in how to calculate the amount of methionine that can be used in feed given to organic poultry while the industry searches for an alternative, a matter the board voted on Friday to send back to committee to determine a solid deadline for the phase out of the material.

"Consumers expect that the sweet happy little chickens have been out there on the little family farms" running around a pasture, said Jean Richardson, an organic consultant who also serves on the board. However, that's not entirely possible given the consumer demand for cheap food. Consumers want large eggs and large chickens, and the fast growing lines bred to produce those, even in organic production, require huge amounts of nutritional inputs.

---

*Debates also are raging in the organic industry over how to handle dairy cows that initially were raised on conventional farms and what to require of organic aquaculture.*

---

"At the moment I actually don't think we have much choice" but to allow for the continued use of synthetic methionine "if we really want to meet consumer demand" for organic poultry, Richardson added.

The board also was petitioned to grant a three-year extension for the approved use of streptomycin, which has helped organic apple and pear growers stave off fire blight, giving them more time to transition to non-antibiotic alternatives. The board narrowly voted, 8-7, to favor the extension. The measure failed, however, as the count did not meet the NOP's two-thirds majority requirement on such votes. As a result, growers now have until October [2014] to phase out their use of the antibiotic.

Harold Austin, director of orchard administration for the Zirkle Fruit Company and one of the NOSB members, had argued during the board's discussion of the issue Tuesday to allow more time to find alternatives and let "science run its course."

Debates also are raging in the organic industry over how to handle dairy cows that initially were raised on conventional farms and what to require of organic aquaculture, where the USDA is working on standards. Some organic advocates are skeptical the organic label can be applied legitimately to seafood.

But the old guard and the big new players in the organic industry do agree on one thing when it comes to debating the rules surrounding the USDA's organic seal. They have zero interest in seeing the label's integrity damaged in any way.

"Consumer trust in the field is the most important thing for the long-term viability" of the organic program, said Laura Batcha, executive director of the Organic Trade Association—which counts roughly 1,100 producers among its members, including such titans as Horizon Foods and Earthbound Farm.

"What consumers are concerned about is the minimal list, what is used in organic production and food" that isn't organic, she told POLITICO. The process of how things stay on or come off of the list is less important than "what those decisions are" when the NOSB does take action, and "the definitive impact about the materials in organic production."

"It's really a unique industry," Batcha said. Organic producers "voluntarily choose to participate in a mandatory requirement, so the value of the seal in the market place is where it all starts and stops."

# 10

# Genetically Modified Foods Should Not Be Sold Under the Organic Label

*Dan Glickman and Kathleen Merrigan*

*Dan Glickman is a former congressman and secretary of agriculture from 1995 to 2001; he is the current executive director of the Aspen Institute Congressional Program. Kathleen Merrigan is a consultant and former deputy secretary of agriculture from 2009 to 2013.*

*While under the Organic Foods Production Act genetically modified organisms (GMOs) cannot be used in organic products, these products cannot advertise as "GMO-free." Regulators argue that it's too difficult to ensure produce is GMO-free due to cross-contamination of crops; however, the GMO-free label should apply to all organic products as they are already verified. Confused consumers are demanding GMO-free labeling without realizing they can already avoid GMOs by purchasing organic.*

Many Americans would like to know more about what they eat, including whether the food they purchase contains genetically modified organisms, or GMOs. That desire has sparked ballot initiatives and bitter fights in states across the country. But what a lot of concerned consumers don't realize is that there is already a way to ensure that the foods they purchase are free of GMOs.

During the [Bill] Clinton administration, we were responsible for implementing the Organic Foods Production Act [of 1990]. One of the implementation decisions that had to be made about the law after its passage was whether GMOs could be used in organic food. After receiving nearly 300,000 public comments during the rule making process, we said no. This means that foods certified as organic are also GMO-free.

So why aren't more consumers aware of this? Because producers of organic food are in effect banned from letting them know.

## Label Laws

Personally, neither of us is opposed to the use of GMOs and believe they can address important food and agricultural needs. The public made clear, however, that it didn't feel such organisms belonged in food with an "organic" label.

---

*All told, this year more than half the states considered some sort of GMO labeling measure.*

---

For more than a decade, organic farmers, ranchers and food processors have been subject to rigorous annual inspections to ensure they are in compliance with national organic standards. The scrutiny is carried out by agents accredited by a division of the Department of Agriculture [USDA]. But responsibility for overseeing food labeling lies with another part of the USDA, along with the Food and Drug Administration [FDA], and they continue to reject petitions by organic food producers who want to label their products as "GMO-free" or "produced without use of GMOs."

Absent such labeling, we continue to have expensive election fights. Last month [November 2013], for example, a ballot initiative in Washington state sought to mandate labeling of food produced using genetic engineering. It was narrowly defeated, but only after months of debate and $30 million of spending by those wishing to sway voters one way or the other.

Connecticut and Maine have both passed laws requiring labeling of foods containing genetically modified organisms, although the laws won't go into effect until neighboring states pass similar labeling laws. All told, this year more than half the states considered some sort of GMO labeling measure. Leaders on both sides of this food fight have vowed to carry on.

We believe that much of the energy around GMO food labeling would dissipate if the federal government honored the original deal we struck on organic food and allowed producers to label their products as GMO-free.

Resistance by the USDA seems especially inconsistent, given that one branch of the agency enforces the organic rule, including the GMO prohibition, while down the hall, another rejects labels submitted by organic companies.

For many years, the agency said this was because it had no way to verify such claims. Thanks to Secretary [of Agriculture] Tom Vilsack, who issued a memorandum this year [2013] directing all USDA agencies to recognize the department's organic standards, the verification objections are dying down.

But now there is debate over what a label should say. The FDA published draft guidance on voluntary GMO labeling in 2001 but has never completed its document, leaving the organic industry in limbo. Recently the USDA has indicated a willingness to consider "non-GE" as a potential label claim [GE stands for genetically engineered]. That is the term preferred by the biotechnology industry, but it is unfamiliar to the vast majority of consumers.

Another impediment to labeling cited by regulators is the fact that there are trace amounts of GMOs in the environment, which makes producing an absolutely pure GMO-free food product challenging. But this is reason for industry and government to work harder to find ways to prevent cross-contamination of crops, not sufficient justification to reject GMO-free labels.

There is broad consensus that a threshold for an allowable—and unavoidable—amount of GMOs in organic and other non-GMO produced food is a necessary accommodation. The U.S.-based Non-GMO Project and European countries set this threshold at 0.9%. The USDA and FDA should adopt this threshold and move forward expeditiously.

An organic GMO-free label would also help consumers distinguish organic food from food labeled as "natural." Natural foods are eroding the organic market space, despite the lack of any clear-cut standard for what the term means or federal oversight. Allowing organic products to be labeled GMO-free would provide a clear distinction between the terms "organic" and "natural."

Mandatory GMO labeling of all food will continue to arouse passions on both sides of the issue. Though it may not satisfy all GMO-labeling advocates nor be welcomed by all leaders in the biotechnology industry, allowing a GMO-free organic label provides more choice in the marketplace and responds to the demands of millions of American consumers in a practical and common sense way.

# 11

# Big-Chain Stores Make Organic More Affordable

*Tracie McMillan*

*Tracie McMillan is a Brooklyn-based writer and author of* The American Way of Eating: Undercover at Walmart, Applebee's, Farm Fields and the Dinner Table. *She has written about food and class for a variety of publications, including* The New York Times, The Washington Post, *and* Slate.

*Common wisdom suggests that only the wealthy care about pesticide-free food, but that is not true. Studies show that the low-income population values organic food more highly than the wealthy. It is only the higher price that prevents them from purchasing organic more often. Organic food is now making an appearance at some discount stores, including Walmart, which offers organic foods at a lower price and puts it within reach of more people.*

A man who applies pesticides to Iowa fields for $14 hour might not seem a likely organic enthusiast. But when I met Jim Dreier last fall, and he mentioned the backyard patch he and his wife had planted with vegetables in the spring, he told me he didn't use any pesticides. When I asked him why, Dreier surprised me: "I don't want to eat that shit," he said. When I went grocery shopping with his wife, Christina, she surprised me, too, by picking out a bag of organic grapes even though she was paying with Snap—food stamps [Supplemental Nutrition Assistance Program]—for exactly the same reason.

I thought about Jim and Christina last week, and my surprise at their organic habits, after Walmart announced it will be adding 100 new organic products to its shelves this month [April 2014]. For as long as I can remember, "organic" has been synonymous with affluence and conscious consumption. Partly, that's because organic foods are typically 30% more expensive than conventional items. But part of it is our assumption about who exactly buys organic and why. Typically, it hasn't been families like the Dreiers, who are raising three kids on Jim's $14 an hour and can't really afford it. So we tend to think that people who buy organic food are part of a select group: urban, well-meaning, affluent, educated "foodies".

*As Walmart's market researchers well know, the poor actually do care about organic.*

## Organic Shoppers

This is a pernicious myth. In reality, the poor actually consider organic food *more* important than the rich, according to top researchers—and organic isn't a "select" phenomenon at all. Three-quarters of American shoppers buy organic food at least occasionally and more than a third do so monthly, according to industry analysis by the Hartman Group. When researchers asked why shoppers didn't buy organic more often, two-thirds said it was because of the higher price.

And yet the myth that only the rich buy organic persists, driven by a kind of circular logic that conflates preference (valuing organic) with behavior (actually buying it). The cost of organic food keeps the poorest families from buying it often, and since only the wealthy can easily afford organic food, the only people we see buying it are wealthy. That, in turn, makes organic food into a norm for the rich, and a treat for the rest of us.

Organic enthusiasts rarely help to clarify the situation, with some of the most prominent leaders making painfully tone-deaf comments about shoppers' priorities. In 2008, just as the economy began to tank, respected chef and food advocate Alice Waters argued that shoppers make the choice between organic grapes and "Nike shoes—two pairs", arguably adding to the perception that the poor simply do not prefer organic food.

As Walmart's market researchers well know, the poor actually do care about organic. The biggest supermarket chain in America, Walmart has a customer base among the country's poor and working class. The company estimates that 18% of Snap is spent in its stores, according to a recent series by *Slate* and *Marketplace* on the retailer—enough that it currently lists changes to public assistance programs as a potential liability for investors.

Meanwhile, organic food has been one of the retailer's strongest categories of sales, says *Marketplace*'s Krissy Clark, who reported the Walmart series. "It makes sense to focus on the growth area," she told me recently. And with cuts to public assistance from the farm bill going into effect, Clark added, the new organic line could attract "higher income consumers who are also feeling a squeeze, and maybe have reasons they wouldn't shop at Walmart. This gives them incentive."

While Walmart made a failed bid at going upscale a few years ago, its new organic line might have better luck. That's because the new products will be branded under Wild Oats, a longstanding natural foods brand that Whole Foods bought and then resold in the 2000s. (Whole Foods sold the brand after a federal court ruled the merger violated anti-trust laws.) With the glimmer of brand-name recognition that Wild Oats could inspire, middle- and upper-income shoppers may be persuaded to take a closer look at Walmart. And the prices seem low enough to fit the modest shopper's budget: a can of Whole Foods' 365 organic corn sells for $1.29 at my local Brooklyn store, but Walmart plans to sell Wild Oats vegetables for 88 cents a can.

Where I live, I can pick from Whole Foods and farmers markets, not to mention food cooperatives that offer organic food affordably, so Walmart's move doesn't mean much for folks like me. And precisely what the new line will mean systemwide—how Walmart's massive scale will affect organic farmers and prices throughout the market—remains to be seen. But for families like the Dreiers, who—like an estimated 15% of Walmart's own workers—work hard and yet still need Snap to pay for food, it offers something new: an organic option they can afford. And it reminds me that I never should have been surprised that they'd want one in the first place.

# 12

# Mass-Produced Organic Food Threatens Organic Farming

*April M. Short*

*April M. Short is an associate editor at AlterNet.*

*Walmart's announcement to bring organic foods into its stores was met with mixed responses. Although cheaper, mass-produced organic foods could bring organic to more people, many are concerned that the value of the products will be compromised. It is costlier for the farmer to use organic methods. And they worry that Walmart may seek lower-quality and imported food to meet the demand for low-cost organics. Walmart counters by claiming they will lower costs by streamlining the process between farm and store shelf.*

Mark Smallwood remembers gardening with his grandmother in Ohio when he was a kid. They used organic farming techniques because, to his grandma, that was just how gardening was done.

"I don't think [my grandma] could pronounce the word, 'chemical,'" he said in an email. "Everything we did was organic."

Today Smallwood is the executive director of the Rodale Institute, which works to create new sustainable and organic food production models for the world to follow. Smallwood has watched organic farming evolve and grow over the years, mainly via dedicated small-time farmers in pockets across the country. When Walmart announced [in April 2014] plans to open a new line of super-cheap organic foods, Smallwood's reaction was mixed. Like many Smallwood recognized the potential for Walmart—the nation's biggest grocer—to expand the organic foods model. But, while some food justice advocates have welcomed the move as it promises to make organic foods available to the masses, Smallwood says there is a good reason organics are priced the way they are. He fears lowering the price of organic foods would fail to reflect their true production costs, and Walmart organics could ultimately threaten the greater organic farming world.

After a 20 year career as a basketball coach in Ohio, Smallwood took over an organic farm in Kent, Connecticut.

"I drove oxen instead of using a tractor," he said. "In my last year there, we used about 43 gallons of gas for the entire year."

At the time, this made Smallwood part of a small sector of farmers—many of them "hippies"—who refused to use what they recognized to be harmful chemicals on their crops.

---

*It's no longer the image of a small organic farmer with four acres and a hog. This is mainstream now—this is an industry worth over $31.5 billion.*

---

When he left the farm, Smallwood worked in a small organic market called MOM's (My Organic Market). Then, Whole Foods recruited him to help 40 stores divert their waste from the landfill, and source food locally—a move that was unprecedented at the time.

Smallwood has seen huge expansions in the organic food production, particularly in the last decade. What started as a niche trend is now a booming billion dollar industry, held together primarily by a network of small farms that provide food to local community sources.

"Ten years ago, the organic industry was an $11.7 billion industry," he said. "At the end of 2012 it was up to $31.5 billion. Every year organic sees double digit growth. The growth has been amazing and when we talk with policy makers in [Washington] DC, now, for instance, it's no longer the image of a small organic farmer with four acres and a hog. This is mainstream now—this is an industry worth over $31.5 billion."

## There's a Right Way and a Wrong Way to Do Organic Farming

When you think about it, the term "organic farming" is a misnomer. Really, we should be saying "chemical farming" to describe farming practices that use pesticides and other toxic concoctions, and just plain "farming" to describe organic practices, sans [without] chemicals. Instead, chemicals are the norm in the agriculture world—so much so that farming without them is the weird, "alternative," method with labeling requirements to boot.

Prior to the 1920s, "organic" was the only agriculture because chemical pesticides and soil amendments had yet to be invented. After World War II [1939–1945], researchers figured out that chemicals designed for use as nerve gas during the war could also kill insects. This changed the game. Farmers rushed to get ahold of the new miracle sprays that promised a pest-free crop, year round. Giant commercial farms, today's Big Ag factory farms, developed around the use of pesticides— which they still rely on today.

Studies have, of course, revealed that dousing our food in toxic chemicals isn't by any means benign. According to the Environmental Protection Agency, as well as countless other researchers, chemical pesticides pose significant risks to human health as well as the environment. Pesticides are linked with cancer and other illnesses, and as they seep into the soil they pollute nearby trees and watersheds, and wreak havoc on soil quality as well as animal life. Several animal and insect "pests," (and weeds) have developed resistance to various pesticides, so farmers have increased the pesticide doses. This increases the amount of pesticides that seep into foods that people ingest.

Smallwood noted that growing food with "toxic chemicals, the dominating method, wastes and destroys the soil, which has serious repercussions down the line.

"For every bushel of corn grown conventionally in Iowa, two bushels of soil are lost," he said. "Healthy biological soil sequesters carbon and other greenhouse gases.... In the long run, growing and eating organically contributes to the wellness of our soil, which is the stomach of the Earth. All the biota, the microscopic life in the soil, that's where the nutrient exchange takes place, like in our own gut."

---

*What we see from Big Ag, from the chemical industry, is that the profits are privatized, but the losses are made public.*

---

As early as the 60s some people became skeptical of pesticides and demanded research into their potential hazards. Studies trickled in and stacked up to support the skeptics' concerns. One by one, small-time farmers deserted pesticides for organic methods. This was the birth of the organic farming movement.

At first, only so-called "crunchy, hippie farmers" were growing organic. Organic food is more expensive than nonorganic by nature, because, as Smallwood explains, conventional food is priced artificially low, meaning the prices in the grocery store don't reflect the actual costs.

"What we see from Big Ag, from the chemical [agriculture] industry, is that the profits are privatized, but the losses are made public," he said. "So when the pesticides and herbicides contaminate the local watersheds, and people and animals get sick, and then those chemicals from Iowa wash into the Gulf of Mexico and create a dead zone where nothing can live. Who pays for that? The public. In economics, that's called an 'externality.' If you were to calculate the costs of those cleanups and add them into the cost of conventional food, there would be no comparison."

Today, because they do not dominate the market, the price of organics is prohibitive for many. In recent years "organic" has developed a reputation for being an upscale, elitist option—even a luxury good if you ask Fox News.

"What was once considered 'fringe' is now being called 'elitist,'" said Katherine Paul, director of development and communications for the Organic Consumers Association (OCA).

## Walmart's Plan

In what it claims is an effort to close this gap and bring organics to all, Walmart has teamed up with Wild Oats to produce super-cheap organic foods. The partners promise to save customers "25 percent or more when comparing Wild Oats to national brand organic products."

---

*In order for organic farmers to survive, prices for organic produce should reflect what it actually costs to grow and distribute their food.*

---

While some food advocacy groups are celebrating the Walmart-Wild Oats partnership, people who know the ins and outs of organic production remain largely skeptical.

Paul says while OCA welcomes the greater distribution of organic produce, they caution against the race to the bottom when it comes to pricing.

"Walmart has a history of driving down price to the lowest in the market," she said. "This has proven to be not conducive to producing products the right way, or paying fair wages to those who do produce products using high-quality ingredients and processes."

She said in order for organic farmers to survive, prices for organic produce should reflect what it actually costs to grow and distribute their food.

"We fear that producers, squeezed on price, may resort to substituting high-quality organic ingredients for similar but inferior ingredients, sourced from China, where organic standards are not as rigorous as they are in the US."

Tom Casey, CEO [chief executive officer] of Wild Oats, says the company will collaborate closely with "a select group of manufacturers who share Wild Oats' commitment to making organic products available and affordable," but would not name those manufacturers. He said Wild Oats and Walmart will be able to achieve lower costs by making the supply chain from farmer to consumer more efficient.

"The organic food industry is one of the least efficient product chains. It's highly fragmented throughout the chain," he said in an email. "What we're doing by partnering with Walmart and leveraging their world class distribution is lowering those costs between the farm and consumer. Example: Tomatoes. There are at least five steps involved between the tomato on the farm and the jar of sauce on the shelf. What we're doing will reduce the cost of those steps and bring the product to consumers at a more affordable price."

When asked, Casey did not specify which farms would source its food, but said their focus was on sourcing food in the US as much as possible. They would, however, purchase some of the food internationally.

"We select our manufacturers based on their ability to deliver the highest quality standards required by the Wild Oats brand," he said. "Whenever possible, we source US-based manufacturers; however, in cases where we can't find a domestic partner able to meet quality standards for a particular product or ingredient, we will look outside of the US. At this time, we only have two international partners—one in Italy (pasta) and one in Canada."

## Concerns About Mass-Produced Organics

Smallwood said sourcing food from outside the US could lower the demand from more local organic farming communities.

"[W]e know that whenever Walmart does anything, it has a huge impact," he said. "So they have the opportunity to do good in a major way. But there is a very good reason that organic prices are higher than conventional food."

---

*One of the reasons people are willing to pay more [for organic food] is that they think they're supporting a different ethic ... and that family farmers are being fairly compensated.*

---

When asked to respond to concerns that their partnership could out-price smaller organic farmers, Casey said only that "it's too soon to predict the impact on specific farmers." He insisted their partnership with Walmart is, "overall," a "strongly positive development for organic farming in the US."

In a Rodale News interview, Todd J. Kluger, vice president of marketing for Lundberg Family Farms, called the idea of cutting organic prices by a quarter a "fantasy." Mark Kastel, co-founder of the Cornucopia Institute, said Walmart's cost-cutting drive could undermine the ethical values of organic farming.

"If the company 'Walmart-ed' organics and approached the industry sector as they do in many business lines, this would be quite destructive," Kastel said in the Rodale News interview. "One of the ways they lower price and maximize profits is by focusing on imports and relying on giant, industrial organic factory farms. It's not compatible with organics, which is a values-based and ethics-based industry. One of the reasons people are willing to pay more is that they think they're supporting a different ethic, a different animal husbandry model, and that family farmers are being fairly compensated."

Smallwood encouraged Walmart and Wild Oats to look into the organic food models already in place.

"We hope that Walmart's goal is to build healthy soil that creates healthy food, and ultimately, healthy people," he said. "So if that's what their plan is, that could be good in a very big way. Again, when they do good, they can do a huge amount of good. On behalf of Rodale Institute, we offer our help and guidance to Walmart as they come over to the organic side. We want to welcome them and show them how to do it right."

# 13

## Pesticides Endanger Farmworkers

### Farmworker Justice

*Farmworker Justice is a nonprofit organization that seeks to empower migrant and seasonal farmworkers to improve their living and working conditions, immigration status, health, occupational safety, and access to justice.*

*Pesticide exposure to farmworkers, many of whom are extremely poor with limited resources, account for more injuries and illnesses from chemicals than any other occupation. Immediate symptoms can include blisters, seizures, nausea, breathing difficulties, blindness, and even death. Long term, pesticide exposure is responsible for developmental delays in children, neurological disorders, and cancer. Farmworkers are not given adequate training or protection from the pesticides, and nearby children in schools and day care centers are exposed through drift. Further, the majority of farmworkers have no access to medical care. As consumers become more aware of the risk of pesticides, they should remember the farmworkers who are exposed to much greater concentrations of the chemicals.*

A growing number of US consumers have reduced their consumption of produce grown with pesticides to protect their family's health. Despite increased demand for food grown without pesticides, conventional growing practices dominate agriculture production. Little is being done to protect the farmworkers who are routinely exposed to high levels of toxic pesticides in the fields where they work and in the communities where they live. They can be exposed at levels hundreds of times greater than consumers' exposures to pesticides.

There is an estimated 5.1 billion pounds of pesticides applied to crops each year, and thousands of farmworkers experience the effects of acute pesticide poisoning, including headaches, nausea, shortness of breath, or seizures. Pesticide exposure leads to chronic health problems, such as cancer, infertility (and other reproductive problems), neurological disorders, and respiratory conditions. This report describes the impact of agricultural pesticides on farmworkers and their families and recommends approaches to reduce the unacceptably high rate of pesticide-related injuries, illnesses, and deaths.

*To develop more effective approaches for protecting farmworkers from pesticides, more research about pesticide use, pesticide-related illnesses, and education is needed.*

## Current Protections Insufficient

The Worker Protection Standard (WPS) issued by the U.S. Environmental Protection Agency (EPA) is the primary set of federal regulations aimed at protecting farmworkers from the hazards of working with pesticides. It has not been updated in over 20 years and has not been effective in preventing workers' exposures to toxins in the fields. Over a decade ago, EPA admitted that even when there is full compliance with the WPS, "risks to workers still exceed EPA's level of concern." It is critical that the WPS regulations be revised without further delay to prevent the detrimental effects of pesticides experienced by farmworkers and their families. The WPS must be revised to reflect the inadequate information workers currently have about pesticide hazards and to require increased safeguards for workers from pesticide exposure. Pesticide labels containing information about exposure hazards and precautions (such as protective gear) are only in English, and thus, obscure safety information from most farmworkers.

Any meaningful revisions to pesticide safety laws must account for the multitude of ways that farmworkers and their families are exposed to these chemicals. They should require employers to offer the most up-to-date methods for the prevention of pesticide exposure to workers and their families. Where medically possible, employers should offer workers the option of blood tests to assess pesticide exposure levels. Farmworker children should be protected from dangerous pesticides that drift onto their homes, schools, and parks. No-spray buffer zones between such areas and adjoining agricultural fields would minimize such exposures.

To develop more effective approaches for protecting farmworkers from pesticides, more research about pesticide use, pesticide-related illnesses, and education is needed. Lack of information hinders public health officials, occupational safety experts, medical personnel, employers, and consumers from making decisions that would best protect farmworkers from pesticide exposure. Data on pesticide use in the United States is insufficient. Only a few states require pesticide applicators to provide regulatory agencies with the name, amount, or location of the pesticide used. Data on pesticide-related illnesses are equally inadequate. Many states do not require healthcare providers or public health officials to report pesticide-related illnesses, and there is no national monitoring system for exposure-related injuries. Most healthcare providers receive minimal training on the identification, diagnosis, and treatment of pesticide-related illnesses. There are few clinical diagnostic tools to confirm pesticide overexposure. There is also little information on the impact of pesticides on farmworker health. More research and data are needed on several issues-determining safeguards for pesticides, medical care for injured workers, and safety precautions for employers. . . .

## Regular Pesticide Exposure

In July 2005, a crew of farmworkers was poisoned in an onion field in Caldwell, Idaho. During the night, a crop duster had applied three pesticides to the field but had not notified the farm owner. At 6:30 a.m., a crew of 29 workers began weeding the field that had not been posted with warning signs. They noticed that their clothes became wet as they worked but they believed the liquid was just dew. By noon, several workers were vomiting and suffering from headaches, nausea, and diarrhea.

---

*Pesticide exposure causes farmworkers to suffer more chemical-related injuries and illnesses than any other workforce nationwide.*

---

Many continued to weed the field, not realizing that their symptoms were the result of pesticide exposure. Many of them were new workers and had not received pesticide safety training from their employer as required by federal law. Workers continued to become ill, vomiting and too weak to stand. Their supervisor gave them lemons in an attempt to reduce the nausea. Eventually, everyone stopped working and left the field. Someone made an emergency call, and an ambulance arrived. Local firefighters responding to the call set up a decontamination tent next to the field for clothing removal and washing. In all, 22 workers were hospitalized. Two were admitted to the hospital for critical care. Two weeks after the exposure, the Idaho Department of Agriculture reported the names of the pesticides used: methomyl, cypermethrin, and mancozeb. The Environmental Protection Agency (EPA) includes methomyl in the highest toxicity category for pesticides (Category 1). The farm was fined for failure to train employees properly and failure to provide and maintain proper safety information at a central location on the farm.

More recently, on December 21, 2012, a crop duster sprayed pesticides over 40 farmworkers working in a Yuma, Arizona farm field. Firefighters responding to the incident decontaminated the workers by having them remove their clothes in the cold night air and sprayed them with a fire hose. The workers complained of irritation to the eyes, nose, throat, and skin. Ten workers were treated at a local hospital. Sadly, incidents like these are not uncommon because farmworkers are not afforded adequate workplace protections from pesticide exposure. While these cases are noteworthy for their attention in the news media, many more incidents go unreported in the press and even to appropriate authorities.

Pesticide exposure causes farmworkers to suffer more chemical-related injuries and illnesses than any other workforce nationwide. Occupational exposure to pesticides poisons as many as 20,000 farmworkers every year, according to estimates by the EPA. The numbers are likely much higher. Several factors contribute to the underestimation of the problem, including the inability and apprehension of affected workers to get medical care, medical misdiagnosis, and the absence of a coordinated national incident reporting system.

---

*Pesticide exposure is an unavoidable reality for farmworkers and their families because pesticides are in the air they breathe, the water they drink, the food they eat, and the soil they cultivate.*

---

Farmworkers are exposed to pesticides in a variety of ways. Workers who perform hand labor tasks in treated areas risk exposure from direct spray, aerial drift, or contact with pesticide residues on the crop or soil. Workers who mix, load, or apply pesticides can be exposed to pesticides due to spills, splashes, and defective, missing or inadequate protective equipment.

Even when not working in the fields, farmworker families, especially children, are also at risk of elevated pesticide exposure. Workers bring pesticides into their homes in the form of residues on their tools, clothes, shoes, and skin. They inadvertently expose their children through a hug if they cannot shower after work. The close proximity of agricultural fields to residential areas results in aerial drift of pesticides into farmworkers' homes, schools, and playgrounds. Some schoolyards are directly adjacent to fields of crops that are sprayed with pesticides.

Pesticide exposure is an unavoidable reality for farmworkers and their families because pesticides are in the air they breathe, the water they drink, the food they eat, and the soil they cultivate.

## Health Impacts of Pesticide Exposure

Farmworkers suffer serious short- and long-term health risks from pesticide exposure. Short-term (acute) effects may include stinging eyes, rashes, blisters, blindness, nausea, dizziness, headaches, coma, and even death. Some long-term health impacts are delayed or not immediately apparent such as, infertility, birth defects, endocrine disruption, neurological disorders, and cancer.

> *Most farmworkers do not receive adequate medical care for work-related injuries or illnesses.*

Rural and agricultural communities have been found to experience higher rates of leukemia, non-Hodgkin lymphoma, multiple myeloma, and soft tissue sarcoma, as well as cancers of the skin, lip, stomach, brain, and prostate. Workers who reported farm work as their primary occupation suffered elevated risks for prostate cancer, esophagus cancer, and oral cavity cancers.

The risks posed by pesticide exposure are exacerbated by the vulnerability of migrant and seasonal farmworkers and their communities. Most farmworkers are poor immigrants with limited formal education. Many do not speak English fluently, and most are isolated in rural areas far from supportive networks and services. An estimated 60% of the nation's 2.5 million farmworkers and dependents live in poverty. Most farmworkers (88%) are Hispanic. Others are African-American, West Indian, Southeast Asian, White, and Native American. Approximately 20% of all hired farmworkers are women and approximately 12% are adolescents. A majority of farmworkers lack legal work authorization. This makes them unlikely to report violations of workplace safety laws, to report abuse of other protective regulations, and unlikely to seek medical attention or report poisonings.

Most farmworkers do not receive adequate medical care for work-related injuries or illnesses. Less than 20% of hired farmworkers receive employer-provided health insurance. The majority of states require no or limited workers' compensation insurance coverage for agricultural workers who suffer occupational injuries or illnesses. When such coverage exists, barriers to access deny many farmworkers the medical services and wage-loss benefits that they are owed. The risk of employer retaliation discourages many farmworkers from seeking medical treatment or from challenging illegal or unsafe pesticide practices.

Barriers to medical care for pesticide illness for farmworkers and their families include lack of health insurance, language barriers, immigration status, and lack of transportation. Many farmworkers live in remote, rural areas at a significant distance from health clinics and even further away from a hospital or urgent care center. Federally-funded migrant health centers provide primary care on a low-cost sliding fee scale, but only about 20% of eligible farmworkers and their families take advantage of such clinics. Since few seasonal farmworkers receive paid sick leave, going to the doctor can be a costly endeavor. . . .

## Reducing Pesticide Exposure

Farmworkers and their families are exposed to pesticides on a daily basis, in large quantities and over sustained periods. Consumers have become aware of the risks that pesticides pose to their health. We should not continue to ignore the dangers such exposures pose to farmworkers' health, in both the short and long term.

Achieving effective and comprehensive protections against occupational pesticide exposure for farmworkers requires swift and sustained action by the federal government. To accomplish this goal, the following recommendations are suggested.

*Give farmworkers and their families the information they need to protect themselves from pesticides.* The WPS should be revised and strengthened. The EPA has delayed issuing revisions to the WPS for far too long.

• Revisions should include: (1) improved and more frequent safety training for workers, (2) a method of verifying comprehension of the information, (3) improved hazard communication about the specific pesticides they are exposed to (including short- and long-term impacts of exposure), and (4) more meaningful enforcement mechanisms to prosecute those who put workers' lives at risk.

• Require Spanish translations on pesticide labels to ensure that this information can be quickly and accurately explained by supervisors and accessed by workers who have questions about proper usage and safety precautions.

• Federal and state agencies should work more closely with farmworker organizations to develop effective educational materials and to ensure that workers are fully informed of the dangers posed by pesticides, understand how to protect themselves and their families, and can exercise their right to a safe workplace.

*Demand better information about farmworkers' pesticide exposures and implement stronger protections for workers and their families.*

• Require reporting of pesticide use and pesticide poisoning incidents on a national level. Such information is necessary to make important decisions regarding medical treatment, public health, and pesticide regulation.

• Require medical monitoring of workers who regularly handle neurotoxic pesticides to identify overexposures before there is irreversible harm and to understand the human health effects of exposure.

• Impose no-spray buffer zones around homes, schools, parks, and other areas where farmworker families can be exposed to dangerous pesticides that are prone to aerial drift.

• Expand research on the long-term impacts of pesticides to farmworker health, on measures to reduce farmworkers' exposure to pesticides, and on safer alternatives to pesticides.

Participants throughout the entire food system need to recognize their responsibility for reducing preventable injuries, illnesses and deaths from pesticides. Supermarket chains, food service companies and other institutional purchasers of produce should collaborate with farmworker organizations and growers to reduce health risks to farmworkers and consumers. In addition to taking voluntary action, these entities should support stronger governmental protections and oversight to assure that our food supply is safe for consumers and for the people who labor on our ranches and farms.

# 14

# Workers on Organic Farms Are Not Always Paid Fairly

*S.E. Smith*

*S.E. Smith is a writer and editor based in northern California.*

*The organic label is not a guarantee that the farmworkers who grew the product were treated ethically. Often the work on organic farms is not much different than on large conventional, factory farms. Workers still face pesticide residue, sub-par housing, low wages, and harsh treatment. Small farms that can't afford the organic certification but treat their employees, community, and environment with respect may be the more conscientious choice for consumers.*

Buyers of organic produce actively seek it out because they believe it will be more environmentally sound, sustainable, and nutritious. Some may also be operating under the impression that labourers on organic farms receive fair treatment, because that seems like it would go along with the organic ethos; it seems odd to think of exploiting workers to produce foods that are 'ethical,' after all. Yet, many consumers don't conduct a lot of research into the sources of their organic food to determine whether workers actually *are* treated fairly, and the scene on organic farms can be just as bad as it is on conventional ones.

## What 'Organic' Doesn't Mean

It is important to be aware of what the organic label is and is not. Rooted in the idea that it is important to move away from petroleum-based pesticides, herbicides, and other crop treatments, the label places restrictions on how food can be grown and what kind of conditions can be present on farms. This doesn't mean that crops are never treated, however; copper sulfate is widely used on organic farms, for instance, and it can cause poisoning if it is applied by workers without adequate protections.

Furthermore, materials used for mulching on organic farms can contain residue from spraying conventional crops, something some farms may actually take advantage of as a management strategy. By using sprayed material for mulch, they can cut down on infestations while still legally meeting the organic standard. Mulch can also include bone meal and refuse from slaughterhouses; so much for organic vegetables being vegetarian. Soy in particular, as a heavy feeder crop, is almost always grown with help from animal products.

---

*Many people are not educated about the facts behind the organic label.... There's no requirement to, for example, protect the soil, let alone treat workers fairly and honestly.*

---

And, of course, organic farms are not necessarily small. 'Organic' may draw a picture of a quiet, sleepy farm with nice folksy people handling the tilling by hand. Industrial organic, however, is the name of the game; organic farms are just as large as their conventional counterparts, they use the same heavy equipment and aggressive techniques, and they also rely heavily on a pool of maltreated labourers, many of whom work for poor wages, in harsh conditions, without even basic protections like masks to wear while spraying.

Most organic farms in California do not pay a living wage or offer any kind of benefits, just like their conventional counterparts. Workers complain of the same problems seen on conventional farms, including wage theft, forced labour, long working hours, unsafe conditions, and favouritism from supervisors. The bottom line is that people want and expect cheap food, and treating workers fairly makes food more expensive. Many organic workers can't even afford to buy the crops they grow and harvest, and have difficulty meeting the needs of their families.

This doesn't sound very much like food justice. In fact, it sounds like the opposite of food justice, which is notable coming from farms that are directly profiting from the way they position themselves: as ethical companies producing foods consumers can feel good about eating. Many people are not educated about the facts behind the organic label, and are unaware of what they are really buying when they purchase foods in the belief that they are ethical. Foods carrying this certification aren't genetically modified, and aren't treated with petroleum-based products (for the most part, with a growing list of exceptions), but that's it. There's no requirement to, for example, protect the soil, let alone treat workers fairly and honestly.

And, of course, organic certification has become commodified. It's expensive to get and maintain, which means many small farms cannot afford it, even though they use practices more in keeping with the original tenets of the organic movement. In fact, they're often working in a beyond organic fashion, because they consider more than the chemicals they do and don't use and the genetics of their crops; they think about the community, their workers, the soil, the environment. Uneducated consumers just look for the 'organic' label, though, which means they bypass products from these farms under the mistaken impression that their offerings aren't as ethical or environmentally sound.

Farmers resist calls for better labour practices in part because they argue they are too expensive, and also because of the belief in agricultural exceptionalism, which has been (and is) used to justify abuses in the industry:

> In this respect, organic farmers join most other growers and agricultural industry boosters who use the discourse of agricultural exceptionalism, which is the idea that the agricultural sector is culturally different and deserves to be exempt from the labor standards of other industries. Agricultural exceptionalism, which favors farmers at the expense of farm workers, has historically guided national and state policy. The ideology also pervades the organic and sustainable agriculture movements, which tend to conceptualize social justice as justice for farmers, not farmworkers.

Farm workers deserve food justice too; not just access to fresh, healthy, safe food, but also the right to work in safe, healthy, clean conditions. Organic or not, farm workers shouldn't have to rely on horse troughs for water, be unable to afford the crops they produce, or live in filthy conditions provided by employers who may well charge for the 'privilege' of being housed on the farm. And consumers need to start being more aggressive when it comes to demanding better conditions for workers, because organic food produced by exploited workers is not at all ethical.

The Food Justice Certified label is taking this issue on, creating a method for evaluating farms to certify them as worker-friendly. It's a good start, especially if consumers start looking for it and asking for it, sending a signal to farms that worker abuses will not be tolerated. Here's hoping it isn't diluted the way the organic label was.

# Organizations to Contact

*The editors have compiled the following list of organizations concerned with the issues debated in this book. The descriptions are derived from materials provided by the organizations. All have publications or information available for interested readers. The list was compiled on the date of publication of the present volume; names, addresses, phone and fax numbers, and e-mail and Internet addresses may change. Be aware that many organizations take several weeks or longer to respond to inquiries, so allow as much time as possible.*

**Academy of Nutrition and Dietetics**
120 S. Riverside Plaza, Suite 2000, Chicago, IL 60606
(800) 877-1600
website: www.eatright.org

The Academy of Nutrition and Dietetics is the world's largest organization of food and nutrition professionals. The aim of the Academy is to improve the nation's health and advance the profession of dietetics through research, education, and advocacy. The organization focuses on food and nutrition research and offers scholarships and awards. Its website, EatRight.org, contains numerous papers on managing a healthy, nutritionally sound diet with reviews of current diet trends and facts on organic options.

**California Certified Organic Farmers (CCOF)**
2155 Delaware Ave., Suite 150, Santa Cruz, CA 95060
(831) 423-2263 • fax: (831) 423-4528
e-mail: ccof@ccof.org
website: www.ccof.org

California Certified Organic Farmers (CCOF) supports and promotes organic farming through certification and education. CCOF also advocates for organic interests to ensure national legislation governing food and agricultural policy supports the organic sector, including working toward a farm bill that would help organic farmers receive US Department of Agriculture services and support. The group's website contains recent issues of the *Certified Organic* magazine along with press releases and fact sheets.

## Only Organic
1436 U St. NW, Suite 205, Washington, DC   20009
(202) 688-5834
website: www.onlyorganic.org

The aim of Only Organic is to cultivate a better understanding of what the organic label means and the environmental and health benefits choosing organic provides. This is achieved through the group's website, which contains numerous educational resources including video clips; articles covering breaking news; a blog; organic certification information; organic farming practices; and lists of producers of organic products, retailers, farm markets, and organizations that support organic practices.

## Organic Center
The Hall of the States, 444 N. Capitol St. NW, Suite 445A
Washington, DC   20001
(802) 275-3897
e-mail: info@organic-center.org
website: http://organic-center.org

The mission of the Organic Center is to convene credible, evidence-based science on the environmental and health benefits of organic food and farming and communicate this information to the public. The Center aims to use this information to advance the conversion of agriculture to organic, sustainable methods, improved health for the earth and its inhabitants, and greater awareness of and demand for organic products. Videos produced by the Organic Center along with a monthly blog and newsletter, fact sheets, scientific resources, recipes, and information about its projects are all available on the website.

## Organic Consumers Association (OCA)

6771 S. Silver Hill Dr., Finland, MN 55603
(218) 226-4164 • fax: (218) 353-7652
website: www.organicconsumers.org

The Organic Consumers Association (OCA) is a grassroots organization campaigning for health, justice, and sustainability. OCA deals with issues of food safety, industrial agriculture, genetic engineering, children's health, corporate accountability, fair trade, environmental sustainability, and other key topics. OCA produces a weekly e-mail publication, *Organic Bytes*, as well as a semiannual newsletter, *Organic View*, both of which are available on its website. The site also contains information on local food and farm politics.

## Organic Farming Research Foundation (OFRF)

303 Potrero St., Suite 29-203, Santa Cruz, CA 95060
(831) 426-6606 • fax: (831) 426-6670
e-mail: info@ofrf.org
website: www.ofrf.org

The mission of the Organic Farming Research Foundation (OFRF) is to foster the widespread adoption and improvement of organic farming systems. To that end, OFRF works to support the success of organic farmers through four areas of focus—government policy, education at the university level, research grants, and community building. Its website contains educational material for kindergarten through college students, beginning and transitioning farmers, and the general public.

## Organic.org

753 S. Walnut St., Boise, ID 83712
(208) 331-1244
e-mail: info@organic.org
website: www.organic.org

The mission of Organic.org is to educate people on the benefits of organic agriculture, food, and products. To that end, the organization's website includes clarifying information on what the word "organic" means, what type of products are available, the significance of purchasing organic, and, finally, how to take steps toward an organic lifestyle. Its website also includes an area for kids and a link to subscribe to the Organic.org newsletter.

### Organic Trade Association (OTA)

28 Vernon St., Suite 413, Brattleboro, VT    05301
(802) 275-3800 • fax: (802) 275-3801
website: www.ota.com

The Organic Trade Association (OTA) is a business association for the organic industry in North America. OTA's mission is to promote and protect organic trade to benefit the environment, farmers, the public, and the economy with the goal of seeing organic products enhance people's lives and the environment. OTA represents businesses across the organic supply chain and addresses all things organic, including food, fiber/textiles, and personal care products. You can find press releases, current news and commentary, as well as information on market trends, environment, nutrition, antibiotic use, genetic engineering, food safety, and more on its website.

### Sustainable Food Trade Association (SFTA)

49 Race St., New Castle, VA    24127
(413) 624-6678
e-mail: info@sustainablefoodtrade.org
website: www.sustainablefoodtrade.org

The Sustainable Food Trade Association (SFTA) helps North American organic food member companies implement innovative and sustainable business practices to reduce the impact of industry on workers and the environment. The mission of SFTA is to build the capacity of the organic food trade to transition to sustainable business models. SFTA member support includes industry education via webinars, workshops, articles, and presentations. Links to information on events as well as news updates, conference archives, and press releases are available at its website.

## US Department of Agriculture (USDA)

1400 Independence Ave. SW, Washington, DC   20250
(202) 720-2791
website: www.usda.gov

The US Department of Agriculture (USDA) is the government agency tasked with setting the standards for US organic products and overseeing organic farms and businesses. Other mission areas of the USDA include farm and foreign agriculture services; food, nutrition and consumer services; food safety, marketing and regulatory programs; natural resources and environment; research, education, and economics; and rural development. Information on the requirements for organic farms and businesses is available on the USDA website.

## US Environmental Protection Agency (EPA)

1200 Pennsylvania Ave. NW, Washington, DC   20460
(202) 272-0167
website: www.epa.gov

The mission of the US Environmental Protection Agency (EPA) is to ensure that all Americans are protected from significant risks to human health and the environment where they live, learn, and work. The EPA assists the USDA by assuring USDA policies are implemented with regard to organic claims made by registered pesticide products. Additionally, the EPA develops and enforces regulations, gives grants, studies environmental issues, forms sponsor partnerships, teaches people about the environment, and publishes related information via its website.

## US Food and Drug Administration (FDA)

5100 Paint Branch Pkwy., College Park, MD   20740
(888) 463-6332
website: www.fda.gov

The US Food and Drug Administration (FDA) is the government agency responsible for ensuring the quality and safety of all food and drug products sold in the United States. As such, the FDA regulates safety and truthful labeling of all food products, including dietary supplements (except for livestock and poultry, which are regulated by the US Department of Agriculture), venison and other game meat, bottled water, food additives, and infant formulas. FDA reports and current information on food quality issues are available on its website.

# Bibliography

## Books

Charlotte
Biltekoff

*Eating Right in America: The Cultural Politics of Food & Health.* Durham, NC: Duke University Press, 2013.

Robert J. Davis

*Coffee Is Good for You: From Vitamin C and Organic Foods to Low-Carb and Detox Diets, the Truth About Diet and Nutrition Claims.* New York: Perigee Trade, 2012.

Sarah Elton

*Consumed: Food for a Finite Planet.* Chicago: University of Chicago Press, 2012.

Barry Estabrook

*Tomatoland: How Modern Industrial Agriculture Destroyed Our Most Alluring Fruit.* Kansas City, MO: Andrews McMeel Publishing, 2011.

Jeff Gillman

*How the Government Got in Your Backyard: Superweeds, Frankenfoods, Lawn Wars, and the (Nonpartisan) Truth about Environmental Policies.* Portland, OR: Timber Press, 2011.

Katherine
Gustafson

*Change Comes to Dinner: How Vertical Farmers, Urban Growers, and Other Innovators Are Revolutionizing How America Eats.* New York: St. Martin's Griffin, 2012.

| | |
|---|---|
| Peter Laufer | *Organic: A Journalist's Quest to Discover the Truth Behind Food Labeling.* Guilford, CT: Lyons Press, 2014. |
| Jeanne Nolan | *From the Ground Up: A Food Grower's Education in Life, Love, and the Movement That's Changing the Nation.* New York: Spiegel & Grau, 2013. |
| Kristin Ohlson | *The Soil Will Save Us: How Scientists, Farmers, and Foodies Are Healing the Soil to Save the Planet.* Emmaus, PA: Rodale Books, 2014. |
| Robert L. Paarlberg | *Food Politics: What Everyone Needs to Know.* New York: Oxford University Press, 2010. |
| John Robbins | *The Food Revolution: How Your Diet Can Help Save Your Life and Our World.* San Francisco: Conari Press, 2010. |
| Jack L. Roberts | *Organic Agriculture: Protecting Our Food Supply or Chasing Imaginary Risks?* Minneapolis, MN: Twenty-First Century Books, 2012. |
| Heather Rogers | *Green Gone Wrong: How Our Economy Is Undermining the Environmental Revolution.* New York: Scribner, 2010. |
| Pamela C. Ronald | *Tomorrow's Table: Organic Farming, Genetics, and the Future of Food.* New York: Oxford University Press, 2008. |

Eric Schlosser    *Fast Food Nation: The Dark Side of the All-American Meal.* Boston: Houghton Mifflin Harcourt, 2012.

Arran Stephens    *The Compassionate Diet: How What You Eat Can Change Your Life and Save the Planet.* Emmaus, PA: Rodale Books, 2011.

Keith Stewart    *It's a Long Road to a Tomato: Tales of an Organic Farmer Who Quit the Big City for the (Not So) Simple Life.* New York: The Experiment, 2010.

Melanie Warner    *Pandora's Lunchbox: How Processed Food Took over the American Meal.* New York: Scribner, 2013.

## Periodicals and Internet Sources

Alex Apple    "New Help for Organic Farmers," WCAX, July 17, 2014. www .wcax.com.

Roger Cohen    "The Organic Fable," *New York Times*, September 6, 2012.

Tessa Edick    "What Organic Farming Really Means," *Register-Star*, July 10, 2014.

Jonathan A. Foley    "Can We Feed the World and Sustain the Planet?," *Scientific American*, November 2011.

Food and Water Watch    "A Decade of Dangerous Food Imports from China," 2011. http:// documents.foodandwaterwatch.org.

Angelo Gonzalez    "An Organic Summer," *The Battalion*, July 21, 2014. www.thebatt.com.

Cristina Goyanes    "14 Banned Foods Still Allowed in the U.S.," *Shape*, April 29, 2014. www.shape.com.

Twilight Greenaway    "Organic Food: Still More than an Elitist Lifestyle Choice," *Grist*, September 10, 2012. http://grist.org.

Mahamudul Hasan    "Imported Fruits, Food Items Get Entry Without Chemical Tests," *NewAge*, July 16, 2014. http:// newagebd.net.

Julia Haskins    "Large Study Shows Organic Foods Are Safer, Healthier than Nonorganic," Healthline, July 14, 2014. www.healthline.com.

Bridget Huber    "Apple Growers in Mexico Call Foul on Trade with U.S.," *Seattle Times*, July 12, 2014.

Nancy Huehnergarth    "China's Food Safety Issues Worse than You Thought," *Food Safety News*, July 11, 2014.

Susanna Kim    "11 Food Ingredients Banned Outside the U.S. That We Eat," ABCNews, June 26, 2013. http:// abcnews.go.com.

Jill Krasny    "Economist Tyler Cowen Says Organic Foods Are Just a 'Marketing Label,'" *Business Insider*, September 19, 2012. www.businessinsider.com.

Peter Laufer      "Five Myths About Organic Food," *Washington Post*, June 20, 2014.

*Los Angeles Times*      "The Case for Organic Food," September 5, 2012. http:// articles.latimes.com.

Stanley Lubman      "Why Americans Should Worry About China's Food Safety Problems," *Wall Street Journal* blog, May 21, 2013. http://blogs.wsj.com.

Jared Mehre      "Organic Food: The Biggest Scam Since Bottled Water," *The Badger Herald*, September 12, 2012.

Joseph Mercola      "10 American Foods That Are Banned in Other Countries," Mercola.com, July 10, 2013. http://articles.mercola.com.

Katy Neusteter      "The China Challenge: Are Overseas Organic Foods Up to U.S. Standards?," NewHope360.com, September 26, 2012. http:// newhope360.com.

Brian Pedersen      "Organic Farming as a Business Opportunity," *Lehigh Valley Business*, June 30, 2014. www.lvb.com.

Mischa Popoff      "Organic Purists Condemn Millions to Death," *Consumer Affairs*, June 30, 2014.

Joe Satran      "Local Produce Increasingly Preferred to Organic, Consumer Survey Shows," *Huffington Post*, September 26, 2012. www.huffingtonpost.com.

Rick Schmitt
"As More Imported Foods Reach the Dinner Table, Holes Remain in FDA Safety Net," Minnpost.com, June 27, 2014. www.minnpost.com.

Science 2.0
"Organic Farms Boost Biodiversity," June 28, 2014. www.science20.com.

Eric Sorensen
"Major Study Documents Benefits of Organic Farming," *Washington State University News*, July 11, 2014. https://news.wsu.edu.

Erik Stokstad
"Greening the Food Pyramid," *Science*, July 18, 2014.

Melanie Warner
"Our Unsafe Food Supply Is Killing Us," The Daily Beast, March 3, 2013. www.thedailybeast.com.

Tim Worstall
"Maybe WalMart Has Just Killed the Organic Food Market," *Forbes*, April 10, 2014.

# Index

## A

Abortion concerns with pesticides, 25

Acceptable Dietary Intake, 53

Access to Information Act, 39

Acetylcholine disruptors, 34

Adom, K.K., 48

Aerial drift of pesticides, 92

Aggression levels, 25–26

Agricultural exceptionalism, 98

Agricultural Health Study, 23

Agricultural Marketing Service (USDA), 69

Alar (daminozide), 30

Aldicarb, 24–25

American Spirit cigarettes, 59

Amy's Kitchen, 67

*Annals of Internal Medicine* (journal), 15, 61

Antibiotic-free meat, 16

Antibiotic-resistant germs, 15

Antibiotic use, 12, 15, 22

Antioxidants, 47–49

*Applied and Environmental Microbiology* (journal), 21

Archer Daniels Midland (ADM), 58–59

*Archives of Otolaryngology* (journal), 18

Arsenic, 24

Atomic Energy Commission, 59

Atrazine, 23, 24, 26

Attention-deficit/hyperactivity disorder (ADHD), 19, 28, 35

Austin, Harold, 71

Autism, 19, 23, 35

## B

Bahl, Morgan, 50–53

Baron-Cohen, Simon, 23

Batcha, Laura, 71

Benbrook, Charles, 45–49

Beta-carotene (vitamin A), 64

Beyer, Peter, 64

Big Ag, 83

Big-chain stores and organic foods
more availability, 76–79
overview, 76–77
shoppers of, 77–79

Bisphenol A, 23

Borlaug, Norman, 63

Bravata, Dena, 15–16, 61

Brazil, 8

Bunin, Lisa, 69

Bush, George W., 20

## C

California Department of Public Health, 35

Campylobacter poisoning, 9

Canada, 8

Canada Organic Trade Association, 40

Canadian Food Inspection Agency (CFIA), 39–40, 42–44

Cancer/carcinogens, 23–24, 28, 89

Casey, Tom, 85–86

Center for Food Safety, 69